Distribution of Isotopic and Environmental Tracers in Groundwater, Northern Ada County, Southwestern Idaho

By Candice B. Adkins and James R. Bartolino

Prepared in cooperation with the Idaho Department of Water Resources

Scientific Investigations Report 2010-5144

U.S. Department of the Interior
U.S. Geological Survey

U.S. Department of the Interior
KEN SALAZAR, Secretary

U.S. Geological Survey
Marcia K. McNutt, Director

U.S. Geological Survey, Reston, Virginia: 2010

For more information on the USGS—the Federal source for science about the Earth, its natural and living resources, natural hazards, and the environment, visit http://www.usgs.gov or call 1-888-ASK-USGS

For an overview of USGS information products, including maps, imagery, and publications, visit http://www.usgs.gov/pubprod

To order this and other USGS information products, visit http://store.usgs.gov

Suggested citation:
Adkins, C.B., and Bartolino, J.R., 2010, Distribution of isotopic and environmental tracers in groundwater, northern Ada County, southwestern Idaho: U.S. Geological Survey Scientific Investigations Report 2010–5144, 30 p.

Contents

Figures

Tables

Conversion Factors and Datums

Inch/Pound to SI

Multiply	By	To obtain
inch (in.)	2.54	centimeter (cm)
inch (in.)	25.4	millimeter (mm)
foot (ft)	0.3048	meter (m)
mile (mi)	1.609	kilometer (km)

Temperature in degrees Celsius (°C) may be converted to degrees Fahrenheit (°F) as follows:

$$°F=(1.8×°C)+32.$$

Temperature in degrees Fahrenheit (°F) may be converted to degrees Celsius (°C) as follows:

$$°C=(°F-32)/1.8.$$

Datums

Vertical coordinate information is referenced to the North American Vertical Datum of 1988 (NAVD 88).

Horizontal coordinate information is referenced to North American Datum of 1983 (NAD 83).

Altitude, as used in this report, refers to distance above the vertical datum.

Specific conductance is given in microsiemens per centimeter at 25 degrees Celsius (µS/cm at 25 °C).

Concentrations of chemical constituents in water are given either in milligrams per liter (mg/L) or micrograms per liter (µg/L).

Distribution of Isotopic and Environmental Tracers in Groundwater, Northern Ada County, Southwestern Idaho

By Candice B. Adkins and James R. Bartolino

Abstract

Residents of northern Ada County, Idaho, depend on groundwater for domestic and agricultural uses. The population of this area is growing rapidly and groundwater resources must be understood for future water-resource management. The U.S. Geological Survey, in cooperation with the Idaho Department of Water Resources, used a suite of isotopic and environmental tracers to gain a better understanding of groundwater ages, recharge sources, and flowpaths in northern Ada County. Thirteen wells were sampled between September and October 2009 for field parameters, major anions and cations, nutrients, oxygen and hydrogen isotopes, tritium, radiocarbon, chlorofluorocarbons, and dissolved gasses. Well depths ranged from 30 to 580 feet below land surface. Wells were grouped together based on their depth and geographic location into the following four categories: shallow aquifer, intermediate/deep aquifer, Willow Creek aquifer, and Dry Creek aquifer.

Major cations and anions indicated calcium-bicarbonate and sodium-bicarbonate water types in the study area. Oxygen and hydrogen isotopes carried an oxygen-18 excess signature, possibly indicating recharge from evaporated sources or water-rock interactions in the subsurface. Chlorofluorocarbons detected modern (post-1940s) recharge in every well sampled; tritium data indicated modern water (post-1951) in seven, predominantly shallow wells. Nutrient concentrations tended to be greater in wells signaling recent recharge based on groundwater age dating, thus confirming the presence of recent recharge in these wells. Corrected radiocarbon results generated estimated residence times from modern to 5,100 years before present. Residence time tended to increase with depth, as confirmed by all three age-tracers. The disagreement among residence times indicates that samples were well-mixed and that the sampled aquifers contain a mixture of young and old recharge. Due to a lack of data, no conclusions about sources of recharge could be drawn from this study.

Introduction

The sustainability of the groundwater supply in northern Ada County is crucial to support the rapid development of the area. Between 1970 and 2007, the population of Ada County increased 330 percent from 112,230 to 373,406 (U.S. Census Bureau, 2009). This trend is projected to continue. The Community Planning Association of Southwest Idaho (COMPASS) estimates that the population of Ada County will increase to 875,960 by 2040 (Church, 2007). Significant development is planned for northern Ada County, with a proposed 20,000–30,000 residential homes to be constructed over the next 10 years (Church, 2007).

Until recently, the hydrogeology of northern Ada County has not been well understood. Studies commissioned by developers have improved this situation but, as with many technical studies, additional questions have been raised. Among those questions relating to the long-term sustainability of the aquifer system in northern Ada County is the degree to which recent groundwater recharge is present and whether there is zonation related to hydraulic differences within the aquifer. Because previous studies of the groundwater in the area have made limited use of hydrochemistry, a limited general characterization using a variety of analyses may be useful in adding to the current understanding of the groundwater-flow system. Therefore, the U.S. Geological Survey (USGS), in cooperation with the Idaho Department of Water Resources (IDWR), initiated a study to characterize the distribution of isotopic and environmental tracers in groundwater of northern Ada County.

Purpose and Scope

This report describes the initial characterization of the distribution of isotopic and environmental tracers in groundwater of northern Ada County. It includes brief discussions of environmental tracers, how tracers are used to better understand groundwater-flow systems, and the results from this study. Conclusions in this report about the groundwater-flow system are from data collected for this study. Finally, suggestions are proposed for the collection of environmental-tracer data for future studies.

Previous Investigations

The chemistry of groundwater at various depths in northern Ada County has been discussed at length in various reports. Parliman (1982) presented well-inventory and groundwater-quality data for 665 sites in Elmore, Owyhee, Ada, and Canyon Counties, including a large number in northern Ada County. Analyses were done for major ions, nutrients, and bacteria. These data are available through the USGS National Water Information System (U.S. Geological Survey, 2010a).

Mayo and others (1984) discussed water samples collected from shallow and deep aquifers of the Boise Valley and Boise foothills that represented nonthermal and geothermal waters (geothermal is defined by the IDWR as having a temperature greater than 85°F). Samples were analyzed for major ions, oxygen and hydrogen stable isotopes, carbon-13 and carbon-14, and tritium. Geothermal waters tended to have higher Na/Ca ratios than nonthermal water samples; nonthermal and geothermal waters tended to have the same stable isotope signature. Carbon-14 values ranged from 6.6 to 104.6 pmc (percent modern carbon), and tritium was detected in some samples. Estimated mean residence times in waters along the Boise frontal fault ranged from 0 to 17,000 years.

Wood and Low (1988) presented work done as part of the USGS Snake River Plain (SRP) Regional Aquifer System Analysis program. Because the Regional Aquifer System Analysis was a regional study, few samples were collected and analyzed in northern Ada County. The primary focus of this work was to identify the chemical reactions between the aquifer matrix and groundwater that control solute concentrations in the Snake River Plain aquifer system. Radiocarbon analyses were applied to the geothermal system to determine that recharge probably occurred during the Pleistocene.

Mariner and others (1989) collected water samples from 10 geothermal wells and 3 nonthermal-water springs along the Boise frontal fault immediately north of Boise. They analyzed these samples for major ions, oxygen/deuterium, radiocarbon, and dissolved gasses, concluding that all samples were chemically identical to those from the Idaho Batholith. Two systems were identified, and geothermal groundwater recharge was estimated to occur during the Pleistocene, 15,000–30,000 years before present.

Baker (1991) described historical and short-term water levels, and analyzed 10 samples for major ions from 8 wells in the Dry Creek study area. Groundwater was determined to be a calcium-sodium-bicarbonate type, and concentrations of iron (exceeding 0.3 mg/L) and fluoride (as high as 13 mg/L) were high in select samples.

Parliman and Young (1992) described selected well-inventory and water-chemistry data for 718 thermal water wells and springs in Idaho, with about 12 of these in northern Ada County. Analyses included major ions, nutrients, bacteria, trace elements, tritium, oxygen/deuterium, radiocarbon, and sulfur isotopes ($\delta^{34}S$).

Parliman and others (1996) reported analytical results from 903 wells sampled in the Boise River Valley between 1990 and 1995. Sampling was directed primarily toward detecting natural and anthropogenic contamination. Analyses included major ions, nutrients, bacteria, trace elements, radon, volatile organic compounds (VOCs), and pesticides.

Parliman and Spinazola (1998) presented data for 884 groundwater samples (27 in the Boise foothills) collected by the USGS between 1985 and 1996, as well as previous work. Groundwater was classified into three main hydrochemical types: nonthermal water was primarily of calcium-bicarbonate or calcium-sulfate types, and thermal water was primarily a sodium-bicarbonate type. Isotopic and environmental-tracer data were mentioned, but discussion was limited to noting that carbon-14 data was collected only in wells deeper than 500 ft. This water in the nonthermal aquifers was a mixture of young and old waters, and water from five wells in the geothermal system was recharged approximately 15,000–28,000 years before present. The remainder of the report discusses natural and anthropogenic contamination.

Neely and Crockett (1998) presented water-quality data collected from 281 wells (144 shallow, 137 deep, with 250 ft being the dividing depth), including a number of wells in the northern Ada County area. Data include major ions, nutrients, bacteria, trace elements, radon, VOCs, and pesticides. The study included an evaluation of network design, trend analysis of selected constituents, as well as scatterplots and trilinear (Piper) diagrams. Sampling was done as part of the IDWR-USGS Statewide Water Quality Program.

Hutchings and Petrich (2002) sampled 38 wells throughout the Treasure Valley, as part of the Treasure Valley Hydrologic Project. Only one of the wells (TVHP1) is near the northern Ada County area and was analyzed for major ions and tritium. Radiocarbon was analyzed in a subset of 28 wells in the central Treasure Valley, including TVHP1; a carbon-14 correction model based on carbon-13 values was recommended. The youngest waters were found to be adjacent to the Boise foothills, increasing in age towards the western edge of the basin near the Snake River with a corresponding increase in groundwater mineralization.

Hutchings and Petrich (2002) made four major recommendations for further hydrogeochemical work to help define the groundwater flow system. Of these, one is applicable primarily to northern Ada County. This recommendation is to further study recharge along the Boise frontal fault by quantifying the contribution of natural recharge to Boise-area aquifers in this area. Among the techniques suggested were installation of multilevel monitoring wells, additional groundwater-level data, additional geophysical and stratigraphic work, and a recharge-focused geochemistry study.

SPF Water Engineering, LLC (2004) defined two general aquifers in the foothills north of Eagle in northern Ada County, the Willow Creek and the Northern Margin aquifers, which have differing hydrochemical and temperature properties. In the analysis, 10 wells were used: 4 sampled for this study and 6 others sampled by others, including the USGS and the IDWR. Analyses were for major ions and arsenic. A trilinear (Piper) diagram of the 10 wells indicated waters are primarily of calcium-bicarbonate to sodium-bicarbonate types.

Glanzman and Squires (2009) analyzed data previously collected by United Water and consultants between 1991 and 2008 for 84 samples from 43 wells. Completion information from wells was used to assign each sample to one of five primary aquifers or groups. Analyses were for major ions and arsenic, and a number of trilinear (Piper) diagrams were plotted (Piper, 1944). The five aquifers or groups and their hydrochemical type were determined to be: the Pierce Gulch Sand aquifer, calcium-bicarbonate type; Terteling Springs Formation, calcium-bicarbonate to sodium-bicarbonate types; Willow Creek, calcium-bicarbonate and sodium-bicarbonate types; Spring Valley Ranch wells (most likely in the Tertling Springs Formation), multiple types; and Emmett wells (no connection to above mentioned aquifers), calcium-bicarbonate-sulfate and sodium-bicarbonate types.

Schlegel and others (2009) analyzed 111 surface-water and groundwater samples from the Idaho Batholith, Boise frontal fault, and Nampa-Caldwell area (west of Boise) for oxygen and hydrogen isotopes. Selected samples also were analyzed for major ions, tritium, and carbon-13 and carbon-14. Schlegel and others (2009) generated a local meteoric water line for the Boise area from these data, and discussed how potential climate change has affected the sources of recharge to the Boise area.

Description of Study Area

Hydrogeologic Setting and Framework

Northern Ada County is in Treasure Valley in the western Snake River Plain, located between the northern Rocky Mountains physiographic province and the northern Basin and Range Extensional Province (Wood, 1994). The western Snake River Plain is a northwestern-trending graben valley, 28 mi wide and 155 mi long that was formed during the late Cenozoic Period. The general geology of the western Snake River Plain consists of granitic Idaho Batholith basement rock, overlain by 1.6–2.7 mi of Miocene basalt associated with the Yellowstone hotspot, and covered by lacustrine and fluvial sediments (Mitchell, 1981; Wood and Anderson, 1981; Mayo and others, 1984; Wood and Clemens, 2002). The fluvial and lacustrine sediments consist of interbedded gravel, sand, claystone, and mudstone that were deposited on lakeshores in the Snake River Plain during the Miocene and Pleistocene (Squires and Wood, 2001).

The northeastern part of the study area is dominated by mountainous portions of exposed Idaho Batholith (Wood and Clemens, 2002). The Boise frontal fault delineates the contact between the southwestern edge of the Atlanta Lobe of the Idaho Batholith and the northeastern edge of the western Snake River Plain. The frontal-fault area is a zone of northwest-trending high angle normal faults that have resulted in an offset of about 800 ft from the plain (Mayo and others, 1984; Holdaway, 1994). This "buried" fault (Wood and Clemens, 2002), which is apparent on well-logs and seismic-reflection surveys, shows an important contact between the Idaho Batholith and water-bearing sediments in the western Snake River Plain.

High permeability, water-bearing sediments in northern Ada County occur along paleo-river channels, lakebeds, deltas, and alluvial fans (Hutchings and Petrich, 2002). In the western Snake River Plain lies the Pierce Gulch Sand aquifer that is comprised of stratified sand layers interbedded with silt and clay and is believed to be a very productive aquifer (Squires and others, 2007). This large aquifer underlies the cities of Star, Eagle, and Meridian (fig. 1), and it extends to the northwest to at least the city of Payette (Squires and Wood, 2001; Squires and others, 2007). Underlying the Pierce Gulch Sand aquifer is the Terteling Springs Formation aquifer. The Terteling Springs Formation aquifer, described by Wood and Clemens (2002), is comprised of oolitic sand. It is bounded by clays beneath the Pierce Gulch Sand aquifer system to the southwest and by bedrock to the northwest.

The Willow Creek and Dry Creek drainage basins (fig. 1), in the foothills of the Idaho Batholith, were identified as areas of interest for this study. The Willow Creek aquifer is an isolated aquifer in the foothills of the Willow Creek drainage basin, consisting of coarse sands and gravels that overlie granitic and volcanic bedrock of the Idaho Batholith. The Willow Creek aquifer is stratigraphically older and deeper than the Pierce Gulch Sand aquifer (Squires and others, 2007), and it is related to the sand facies of the Terteling Springs Formation. The Dry Creek aquifer is an isolated aquifer comprised of gravels, sands, and silts that occupies the Dry Creek drainage basin in the foothills of the Idaho Batholith (Baker, 1991). Wells sampled in the western Snake River Plain for this study were in the Pierce Gulch Sand aquifer and shallow unconfined, undifferentiated alluvial material overlying the Pierce Gulch Sand aquifer. Because of the complex geology of the area, wells in the western Snake River Plain are defined by the primary water-bearing zone in which the well is completed. Samples in the foothills aquifers were collected from wells completed in the Willow Creek and Dry Creek aquifers; further details about well selection are discussed in sections, "Site Selection," "Sample Collection," and "Quality Control."

For the current study, recharge to the system is assumed to be from infiltration of surface water and precipitation. Since the 1880s, a canal system has diverted water for irrigation from the Boise River through the Treasure Valley.

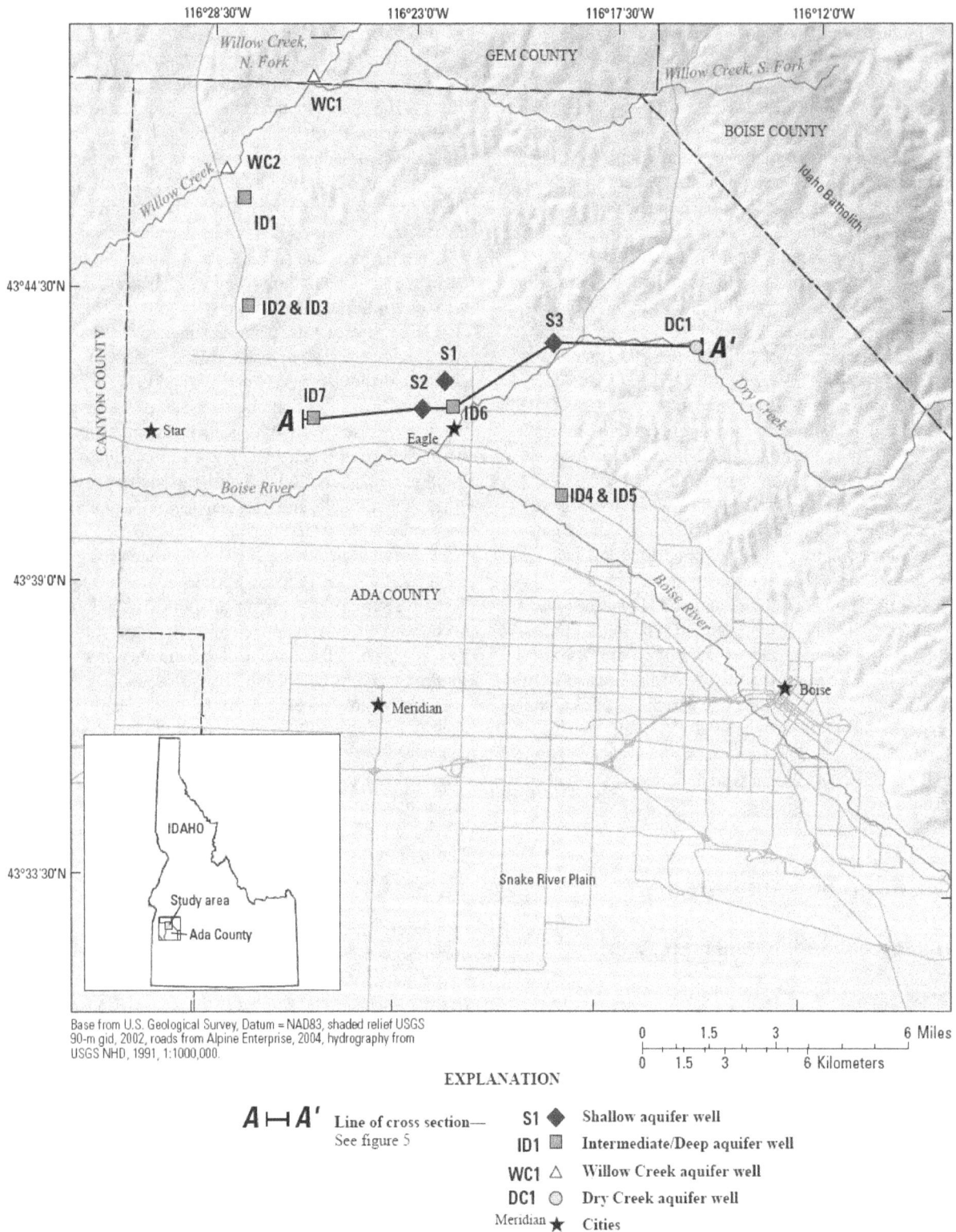

Figure 1. Location of study area and sample well locations, northern Ada County, southwestern Idaho.

About 1,170 mi of major irrigation canals existed throughout the Treasure Valley as of 2004 (Urban, 2004). Canals in the Treasure Valley have been shown to lose significant amounts of water to the groundwater system through seepage (Berenbrock, 1997). Infiltration of precipitation probably only constitutes a small component of recharge; Newton (1991) suggested that only 2 percent of the total annual precipitation in the western Snake River Plain actually recharges groundwater.

Groundwater levels in northern Ada County have been measured for multiple studies. Shallow groundwater in the Pierce Gulch Sand and Willow Creek aquifers moves northwest towards the Payette River Valley (Squires, 2008). Groundwater levels range from a few feet to 397 ft below land surface, depending on the location of measurement and aquifer measured. Groundwater levels in some areas are affected by seepage from local canals and by infiltration from irrigation; mounds near losing portions of the canals are evident in the surface of the water table (Dion, 1972).

Land Use

Land use in northern Ada County is a mixture of sparsely populated rangeland, farmland and rapidly developing suburban and urban areas (the cities of Eagle and Star, fig. 1) (U.S. Department of Agriculture, 2010). Urban development is most dense near the city of Eagle; multi-acre lots are more common farther from the city and in the foothills. In 2000, most land use was classified as rangeland, with the second most common land use being agriculture. The remainder of the land use is classified as residential, commercial, or industrial. Several golf courses exist in the area, as well as a small number of concentrated animal-feeding operations (dairies and feedlots). Residential development has increased significantly in the past 9 years and is projected to continue (U.S. Department of Agriculture, 2010).

Climate

Climate in the study area falls into three classes under a modified Köppen system. The basin floor of the Treasure Valley is classified as BSk, the foothills as Dsa, and the mountains as Dsb. For the valley floor, *BS* indicates an arid steppe climate and *k* indicates that the mean annual air temperature is less than 64 °F. For the foothills, *Dsa* indicates a cold, dry, hot-summer climate; for the mountains, and *Dsb* is a cold, dry, warm-summer climate (Godfrey, 2000; Peel and others, 2007).

The National Weather Service has 78 weather stations within a 50-mi buffer of the study area, although only 37 are active (U.S. Department of Commerce, 2010). Of these 37 stations, 6 are within or immediately adjacent to the study area and have sufficient long-term data for climatic calculations (table 1). As of 2010, two active AgriMet stations are within 25 mi of the study area: Boise, Idaho (BOII) and Nampa, Idaho (NMI) (Bureau of Reclamation, 2006). In addition, two active Natural Resources Conservation Service snow-survey sites are in or adjacent to the study area: one is an instrumented SNOTEL site and the other is a snow course (Natural Resources Conservation Service, 2010).

Table 1.   Climatic data for selected weather stations in and near northern Ada County, southwestern Idaho, 1940–2005.

[Climate data from Western Regional Climate Center (2008). Abbreviations: F, degrees Fahrenheit; in , inches; WSFO, Weather Service Field Office; NAVD 88, North American Vertical Datum of 1988]

Station name and No.	Latitude	Longitude	Air temperature (°F)			Mean total precipitation (in.)	Mean total snowfall (in.)	Altitude (feet above NAVD 88)	Dates in operation	
			Mean July maximum	Mean January minimum	Mean annual				Starting date	Ending date
Boise WSFO Airport (101022)	43 34′N	116 13′W	90.5	22.3	51.2	11.8	19.5	2,860	01-01-1940	12-31-2005
Boise Lucky Peak Dam (101018)	43 33′N	116 04′W	91.6	20.8	51.7	13.7	4.9	2,840	01-12-1951	12-31-2005
Boise 7 N (101017)	43 43′N	116 12′W	87.9	22.7	49.6	19.0	55	3,890	05-01-1973	12-31-2005
Emmett 2 E (102942)	43 52′N	116 28′W	91.5	21.9	51.1	13.4	8.8	2,390	08-01-1948	12-31-2005
Kuna 2 NNE (105038)	43 31′N	116 24′W	88.3	20.2	49.6	9.8	11.9	2,680	08-01-1948	12-31-2005
Nampa Sugar Factory (106305)	43 37′N	116 34′W	91.1	21.5	51.0	11.2	9.6	2,470	10-01-1976	12-31-2005

Long-term means for select National Weather Service stations are listed in table 1. Mean annual air temperatures at the six stations range from 51.7 °F at Boise Lucky Peak Dam to 49.6 °F at Boise 7 N and Kuna 2 NNE. The coldest month in the area is January, with mean low air temperatures ranging from 20.2 °F at Kuna 2 NNE to 22.7 °F at Boise 7 N. Typically, the warmest month is July, with mean high air temperatures ranging from 91.6 °F at Boise Lucky Peak Dam to 87.9 °F at Boise 7 N. Mean total precipitation ranges from 19.0 in. at Boise 7 N to 9.8 in. at Kuna 2 NNE. July and August typically are the driest months; November, December, and January are the wettest (Western Regional Climate Center, 2008).

Methods

Data used for this study were collected from sites specifically selected by the USGS and the IDWR based on location, well depth, well construction, and other criteria. This section provides details about the field methods for site selection, sample collection, and quality-control and laboratory methods.

Field Methods

Site Selection

A total of 15 samples (table 2) were collected for this study during September and October 2009. Of the 15 samples collected, 13 were from domestic, irrigation, monitoring, and municipal wells at 11 sites; 2 were replicate samples collected for quality control. Wells were selected, based on well depth and location, to represent the shallow aquifer, the intermediate/deep aquifer, the Willow Creek aquifer, and the Dry Creek aquifer. Samples from the shallow aquifer were collected from wells at depths less than 60 ft below land surface in the shallow, undifferentiated alluvium of the western Snake River Plain. Intermediate/deep samples were collected from wells at depths ranging from 144 to 425 ft below land surface in the Pierce Gulch Sand aquifer or undifferentiated alluvial aquifers. Willow Creek aquifer samples were collected from wells at depths ranging from 425 to 580 ft below land surface. One sample was collected from the Dry Creek aquifer from a well with a depth of 292 ft below land surface. Well construction and site information are shown in table 2 and well locations are shown in figure 1.

Three samples were collected from the shallow aquifer, seven from the deep/intermediate aquifer, two from the

Willow Creek aquifer, and one from the Dry Creek aquifer (table 2). Two of the seven sites in the deep/intermediate aquifer had wells placed at different intervals that allowed for sampling at two different depths at the same geographical location. Two wells were sampled at each of those two sites (ID2 and ID3, ID4 and ID5). Sample names were assigned based on the aquifer sampled. Replicate (quality-control) samples are listed on all tables for reference underneath the primary sample and are labeled with normal site nomenclature and the letter "R" to indicate a replicate sample.

Sample Collection

At the time of sample collection, a closed path was established between the groundwater source and sampling equipment to prevent contact between sample and air. Where a well had an existing submersible pump, samples were collected as close to the wellhead as possible through existing plumbing. For the four monitoring wells that did not have pumps, a portable electric Grundfos Redi-Flo2® submersible pump and tygon tubing was used.

A Hydrolab® MS 5 multiparameter meter was used to measure specific conductance, pH, water temperature, and dissolved oxygen. The multiparameter meter was connected to the discharge line from the well, and field parameters were recorded before sample collection. Wells were pumped continuously during sample collection. Wells were purged of at least three casing volumes, and field parameters (specific conductance, pH, and water temperature) stabilized before samples were collected.

Samples were collected in appropriate containers and preserved in accordance with the procedures specified in the USGS National Field Manual (U.S. Geological Survey, variously dated). Tritium and physical parameter bottles were rinsed three times with unfiltered water and samples were collected without filtration. Samples for nutrients, metal, major ions, oxygen-18 and deuterium (hydrogen-2), and carbon-13 and carbon-14 were filtered using a 0.45-micron capsule filter. All filtered sample bottles were rinsed three times with filtered water, with the exception of the oxygen-18 and deuterium samples. Chlorofluorocarbon (CFC) and dissolved gas samples were collected using copper tubing. Field procedures followed those outlined by the USGS CFC and dissolved gas guidelines (U.S. Geological Survey, 2006, 2009).

Alkalinity titrations were performed in the field using an incremental titration method. About 60 mL of sample was titrated using 0.1600 N $\pm$ 0.0008 N H_2SO_4 acid through a HACH™ manually operated digital titrator. In addition, specific conductance, pH, and alkalinity were analyzed by the USGS National Water-Quality Laboratory (NWQL).

Table 2.   Site information and well construction for wells sampled in northern Ada County, southwestern Idaho, September and October 2009.

[Sample name: Location of wells sampled are shown in figure 1. Sample names were assigned based on depth and aquifer sampled. Sample names with "R" indicate replicate sample. Depth of well and screening information obtained from well logs associated with USGS well No. Abbreviations: USGS, U.S. Geological Survey; NAVD 88, North American Vertical Datum of 1988; ft, foot; –, no data]

Sample name	USGS station No.	USGS well No.	Latitude	Longitude	Altitude (ft above NAVD 88)	Sample date	Sample time	Depth of well (ft below land surface)	Top of screen (ft below land surface)	Depth to water (ft below land surface)
Shallow aquifer										
S1	434256116215901	04N 01E 05BDAC1	434256	1162159	2,600	09-25-09	1205	43	–	18.0
S2	434224116223501	04N 01E 06DDD1	434224	1162235	2,575	09-24-09	1020	30	–	6.6
S3	434342116190401	05N 01E 34ADCD1	434342	1161904	2,670	09-25-09	1005	54	42	13.3
Intermediate/Deep aquifer										
ID1	434613116273801	05N 01W 16DBC1	434613	1162738	2,730	09-30-09	1140	400	290	216.3
ID2	434412116272704	05N 01W 28DDC4	434412	1162727	2,610	09-23-09	1205	425	–	104.6
ID3	434412116272705	05N 01W 28DDC5	434412	1162727	2,610	09-23-09	1040	144	–	92.3
ID4	434048116184403	04N 01E 14CCB3	434048	1161844	2,582	09-22-09	1150	250	210	1.1
ID5	434048116184404	04N 01E 14CCB4	434048	1161844	2,582	09-22-09	1350	177	130	3.5
ID5R	434048116184404	04N 01E 14CCB4	434048	1161844	2,582	09-22-09	1355	177	130	3.3
ID6	434225116214601	04N 01E 05CDDD1	434225	1162146	2,600	10-30-09	1040	340	183	55.0
ID7	434208116253401	04N 01W 11BDAA1	434208	1162534	2,512	09-24-09	1240	357	270	0.0
Willow Creek aquifer										
WC1	434836116255001	06N 01W 35CCA1	434836	1162550	2,860	09-24-09	1450	580	–	397.1
WC2	434650116280802	05N 01W 09CCD2	434650	1162808	2,680	09-21-09	1320	425	–	334.7
WC2R	434650116280802	05N 01W 09CCD2	434650	1162808	2,680	09-21-09	1325	425	–	334.6
Dry Creek aquifer										
DC1	434343116151601	05N 02E 31ADDD1	434343	1161516	2,765	09-25-09	1440	292	–	85.0

Quality Control

The quality assurance plan practiced at the USGS Idaho Water Science Center (Hardy, 2008) was followed during the collection of water samples for this study. To assure quality control, the multiparameter meter was calibrated in the field before each use and was checked for accuracy at the end of each day. In addition, the multiparameter meter is checked yearly to ensure its accuracy against known reference standards. All field equipment, instruments, and sampling ports were cleaned prior to use. Laboratory protocols for quality control can be found at the various laboratory websites and in the publications listed in section, "Laboratory Methods." No blank samples were collected.

Laboratory Methods

Major Ions and Field Water-Quality Parameters

Major ion, metals, and physical parameters were determined at the USGS NWQL in Denver, Colo. Samples for metals and some major ions were acidified in the field using concentrated nitric acid. Detailed laboratory procedures are described in Fishman and Friedman (1989).

Nutrients

Nutrients were analyzed at the NWQL in Denver, Colo. All samples were collected in 125 mL brown polyethylene bottles and chilled. Laboratory methodologies are described in detail in Fishman (1993).

Oxygen/Deuterium

Oxygen and hydrogen stable isotope samples were analyzed at the USGS Reston Stable Isotope Laboratory in Reston, Va. Samples were collected in 60 mL glass bottles with polyseal caps. Hydrogen-isotope-ratio analyses were performed using the hydrogen equilibration technique (Coplen and others, 1991). Results for stable isotopes are in units of per mil (‰, parts per thousand), and expressed in delta notation (δ) as derived from comparing the sample to the Vienna Standard Mean Ocean Water (VSMOW) standard (Coplen, 1996). The two standard deviation (2-σ) accuracy of oxygen and hydrogen isotope results were 0.2 and 2‰, respectively (Révész and Coplen, 2008a, 2008b).

Tritium

Tritium samples were analyzed by the USGS Isotope Research Laboratory in Menlo Park, Calif. (U.S. Geological Survey, 2010b). Samples were collected in 1,000 mL polyethylene bottles with polyseal cone caps. Samples were treated by electrolytic enrichment and liquid scintillation decay counting methods. The two standard deviation (2-σ) accuracy of tritium results was ±0.3 TU. The minimum detection limit is 0.7 TU. Results were reported by the laboratory in picocuries per liter (pCi/L) and were converted to tritium units for this report using the equation:

$$1\,TU = 3.23\,pCi/L. \qquad (1)$$

Any results indicating a negative tritium activity or activity less than 2 pCi/L were reported as less than 0.7 TU to indicate tritium-dead water.

Radiocarbon

Carbon-isotope samples were analyzed at the National Ocean Sciences Accelerator Mass Spectrometer Facility in Woods Hole, Mass. Samples for carbon isotopes were collected in a safety-coated 1-L glass bottle out of contact with the atmosphere. Carbon dioxide gas was extracted from the sample by acid hydrolysis and reduced to graphite that was made into targets for accelerator mass spectrometry. Process blanks were used for calibration. This method can measure samples as old as 60,000 years with an error of less than 0.4 pmc (Woods Hole Oceanographic Institution, 2003). Results for carbon-14 are reported in pmc, and mean residence times are calculated from the decay equation. Samples reported as "modern" imply that recharge has occurred later than the year 1950 (Woods Hole Oceanographic Institution,

2003). Results for carbon-13 are reported in per mil (‰, parts per thousand) notation, and they are expressed in delta notation (δ) as derived from comparing the sample to the Vienna Pee Dee Belemnite (VPDB) standard (Woods Hole Oceanographic Institution, 2003).

Chlorofluorocarbons and Dissolved Gases

CFCs and dissolved gas samples were analyzed at the Reston Chlorofluorocarbon Laboratory in Reston, Va. Each CFC sample was collected in five 125-mL glass bottles, capped with aluminum foil-lined caps, sealed with electrical tape, and stored upside down. Dissolved gas samples were collected in two 160-mL septum glass bottles and plugged; gasses were allowed to escape during sampling through a hypodermic needle in the septum.

CFC results were determined in the laboratory using the purge-and-tap gas chromatography procedure with an electron capture detector. Dissolved gas samples were allowed to equilibrate with headspace, and the resulting gas was analyzed on a gas chromatograph.

Quality Control

Because method detection limits are low, each analytical method has a corresponding minimum reporting limit. Sample concentrations less than the reporting limit are noted in the tables with the less than (<) sign, and are assumed to be smaller than the laboratory's ability to analyze with certainty. Lower reporting limits are listed beneath each constituent; isotopes, dissolved gases, and CFCs do not have a reporting limit. In addition, samples that have an estimated concentration (denoted as "E" in tables) indicate that results are less than the lowest calibration standard and are only an estimate of the concentration.

Replicate samples were collected at two sites and results are listed beneath the primary sample in all tables. At both sites, the primary and replicate samples were within a 10 percent relative percent difference (RPD) from each other in all constituents using the formula:

$$RPD = [(V_S - V_R)/((V_S + V_R)/2)]*100, \qquad (2)$$

where

V_S is the value of the primary sample, and
V_R is the value of the replicate sample.

For this study, replicate samples were required to fall within a RPD of 10 percent, thus the replicate samples for all constituents indicate that the data are acceptable.

Distribution of Isotopic and Environmental Tracers in Groundwater

Major Ions and Field Water-Quality Parameters

Relations and spatial patterns in water quality resulting from differing flow paths, recharge sources, and the presence of geothermal water are often evident from major ion chemistry and parameters, such as specific conductance, pH, dissolved oxygen, and alkalinity. Such data also may be used to generate trilinear (Piper) diagrams and to define hydrochemical facies (Hill, 1940; Piper, 1944; Back, 1966). Water type as determined by major ion chemistry frequently is used to determine major geochemical reactions occurring in different parts of an aquifer, as well as reactions along a flowpath. This approach has been used by many of the previous geochemical studies in northern Ada County (Neely and Crockett, 1998; SPF Water Engineering, LLC, 2004; Glanzman and Squires, 2009).

Field parameter results varied considerably, depending on the aquifer sampled (table 3). Specific conductance in the samples ranged from 198 to 863 µS/cm; conductivity values were highest in the Dry Creek aquifer (863 µS/cm) and shallow aquifer (470 µS/cm) samples and lowest in the intermediate/deep aquifer and Willow Creek aquifer samples. The pH values of samples ranged from 6.2 to 8.0; pH values were lowest in the shallow aquifer samples and highest in the Willow Creek aquifer samples. Water temperatures ranged from 56 to 85 °F; water temperatures were highest in the Dry Creek aquifer. Dissolved-oxygen concentrations ranged from 0.1 to 9.6 mg/L; dissolved oxygen concentrations typically were higher in the shallow aquifer and intermediate/deep aquifer samples than the Willow Creek and Dry Creek aquifer samples.

Table 3.   Physical parameters for samples collected from selected wells in northern Ada County, southwestern Idaho, September–October 2009.

[Sample name: Location of wells sampled are shown in figure 1. Sample names with "R" indicate replicate sample. Abbreviations: Lab, laboratory;   F, degrees Fahrenheit, µS/cm, microsiemens per centimeter; <, less than]

Sample name	USGS station No.	Specific conductance		pH		Water temperature, field (°F)	Air temperature (°F)	Dissolved oxygen (mg/L)	Alkalinity		Bicarbonate, field (mg/L)	Carbonate, field (mg/L)
		Field (µS/cm)	Lab (µS/cm)	Field	Lab				Field (mg/L as CaCO$_3$)	Lab (mg/L as CaCO$_3$)		
Shallow aquifer												
S1	04N 01E 05BDAC1	198	206	6.8	7.4	58.5	86.0	6.5	90	90	109	<0.1
S2	04N 01E 06DDD1	312	326	6.5	6.8	56.1	73.4	6.4	96	98	118	<0.1
S3	05N 01E 34ADCD1	470	478	6.9	7.2	56.5	67.1	2.1	146	151	178	<0.1
Intermediate/Deep aquifer												
ID1	05N 01W 16DBC1	297	297	6.9	6.9	70.0	48.2	0.1	119	123	145	<0.1
ID2	05N 01W 28DDC4	204	280	7.1	7.1	64.2	78.8	2.6	118	120	144	<0.1
ID3	05N 01W 28DDC5	264	274	6.2	7.1	58.8	77.0	9.6	115	113	140	<0.1
ID4	04N 01E 14CCB3	321	330	7.0	7.3	58.3	68.0	0.1	149	149	182	<0.1
ID5	04N 01E 14CCB4	260	272	6.9	7.3	56.5	73.4	0.1	125	130	153	<0.1
ID5R	04N 01E 14CCB4	264	273	6.2	6.7	58.8	77.0	9.6	115	131	140	<0.1
ID6	04N 01E 05CDDD1	248	259	7.0	7.0	55.9	41.0	5.2	106	112.6	129	0.1
ID7	04N 01W 11BDAA1	232	241	7.1	7.7	63.0	83.3	0.3	104	108	126	<0.1
Willow Creek aquifer												
WC1	06N 01W 35CCA1	244	248	8.0	8.0	85.3	85.1	0.1	77	83	92	<0.1
WC2	05N 01W 09CCD2	219	221	7.0	7.2	74.5	69.8	0.1	104	103	127	<0.1
WC2R	05N 01W 09CCD2	260	221	6.9	7.3	58.3	68.0	0.1	125	103	153	<0.1
Dry Creek aquifer												
DC1	05N 02E 31ADDD1	863	846	7.5	7.9	57.2	89.6	0.9	203	230	247	< 0.1

Major ion chemistry (table 4) indicates that the water types for all samples collected in this study are either a calcium-bicarbonate or a sodium-bicarbonate water type. A trilinear diagram (fig. 2) is used to indicate the water types present in the study area. Water type is determined by calculating the most dominant species in each sample in terms of milliequivalents per liter (meq/L) to give each ion an equivalent weight. The lower right triangle shows calculations for anions, the lower left triangle shows calculations for cations, and the center diamond of the trilinear diagram displays the relation of the seven major species on one diagram. Each point represents one single water analysis and the water type. Water type for shallow aquifer and intermediate/deep aquifer samples were calcium-bicarbonate. The water type of samples from the Willow Creek aquifer and the Dry Creek aquifer was sodium-potassium-bicarbonate, commonly simplified to sodium-bicarbonate due to chemical similarities; therefore, this water type will be labeled as sodium-bicarbonate hereinafter.

Samples also were analyzed for silica, iron, and manganese. Silica concentrations ranged from 36.9 to 52.6 mg/L in shallow aquifer samples, 30.3 to 42.6 mg/L in intermediate/deep aquifer samples, 43.1 to 44.7 mg/L in Willow Creek aquifer samples, and was 55.9 mg/L in the single sample from the Dry Creek aquifer. Iron concentrations in the northern Ada County were less than the detection limit in shallow aquifer samples (less than 4 µg/L), and ranged from less than 4 to 1,020 µg/L in deep aquifer samples. Iron concentrations ranged from 94.2 to 316 µg/L in Willow Creek aquifer samples, and measured 4.8 µg/L in the Dry Creek aquifer sample. Manganese concentrations were less than 0.8 µg/L in shallow aquifer samples. Concentrations of manganese ranged from less than 0.2 to 40.1 µg/L in intermediate/deep aquifer samples and 30.8 to 183 µg/L in Willow Creek aquifer samples. Manganese concentration was 0.8 µg/L in Dry Creek aquifer sample.

Table 4. Major ion and trace metals concentrations for samples collected from selected wells in northern Ada County, southwestern Idaho, September–October 2009.

[Sample name: Location of wells sampled are shown in figure 1. All major ions and trace metals are filtered. Abbreviations: mg/L, milligrams per liter; E, estimated; <, less than]

Sample name	USGS station No.	Calcium (mg/L)	Magnesium (mg/L)	Sodium (mg/L)	Potassium (mg/L)	Chloride (mg/L)	Sulfate (mg/L)	Fluoride (mg/L)	Silica (mg/L as SiO$_2$)	Iron (µg/L)	Manganese (µg/L)
Reporting limit of analyte		0.01	0.006	0.06	0.03	0.06	0.09	0.04	0.1	2	0.1
Shallow aquifer											
S1	04N 01E 05BDAC1	21.1	3.92	14.7	1.84	1.81	6.4	0.25	41.3	E 4	0.3
S2	04N 01E 06DDD1	35.7	8.49	12.3	4.14	15.10	13.9	0.22	36.9	E 3	E 0.2
S3	05N 01E 34ADCD1	53.5	13.70	25.9	3.47	8.68	72.2	0.84	52.6	<4	0.7
Intermediate/Deep aquifer											
ID1	05N 01W 16DBC1	30.7	7.43	19.1	2.28	5.25	25.3	0.55	39.3	1020	13.8
ID2	05N 01W 28DDC4	30.8	5.72	18.0	1.99	3.13	21.3	0.54	32.2	<4	E 0.2
ID3	05N 01W 28DDC5	32.4	5.90	13.9	2.71	4.85	10.5	0.23	42.6	<4	E 0.2
ID4	04N 01E 14CCB3	39.7	7.45	18.8	1.82	2.78	21.2	0.38	31.8	597	40.1
ID5	04N 01E 14CCB4	33.0	4.37	16.8	1.24	3.68	6.6	0.36	30.3	18	14.5
ID5R	04N 01E 14CCB4	32.8	4.34	16.3	1.20	3.69	6.6	0.36	30.3	19	15.3
ID6	04N 01E 05CDDD1	31.1	5.53	14.3	1.58	2.64	12.6	0.41	34.0	6	0.2
ID7	04N 01W 11BDAA1	28.9	5.03	13.8	1.76	2.25	14.1	0.39	31.7	155	3.9
Willow Creek aquifer											
WC1	06N 01W 35CCA1	23.2	0.27	28.3	1.36	4.16	32.1	1.57	43.1	94.2	30.8
WC2	05N 01W 09CCD2	18.2	3.38	21.5	2.29	2.88	6.9	0.29	44.7	316	183
WC2R	05N 01W 09CCD2	18.8	3.50	22.2	2.30	2.87	7.0	0.27	43.4	319	183
Dry Creek aquifer											
DC1	05N 02E 31ADDD1	0.09	E 0.008	1.81	257	6.19	101	0.33	55.9	4.8	0.8

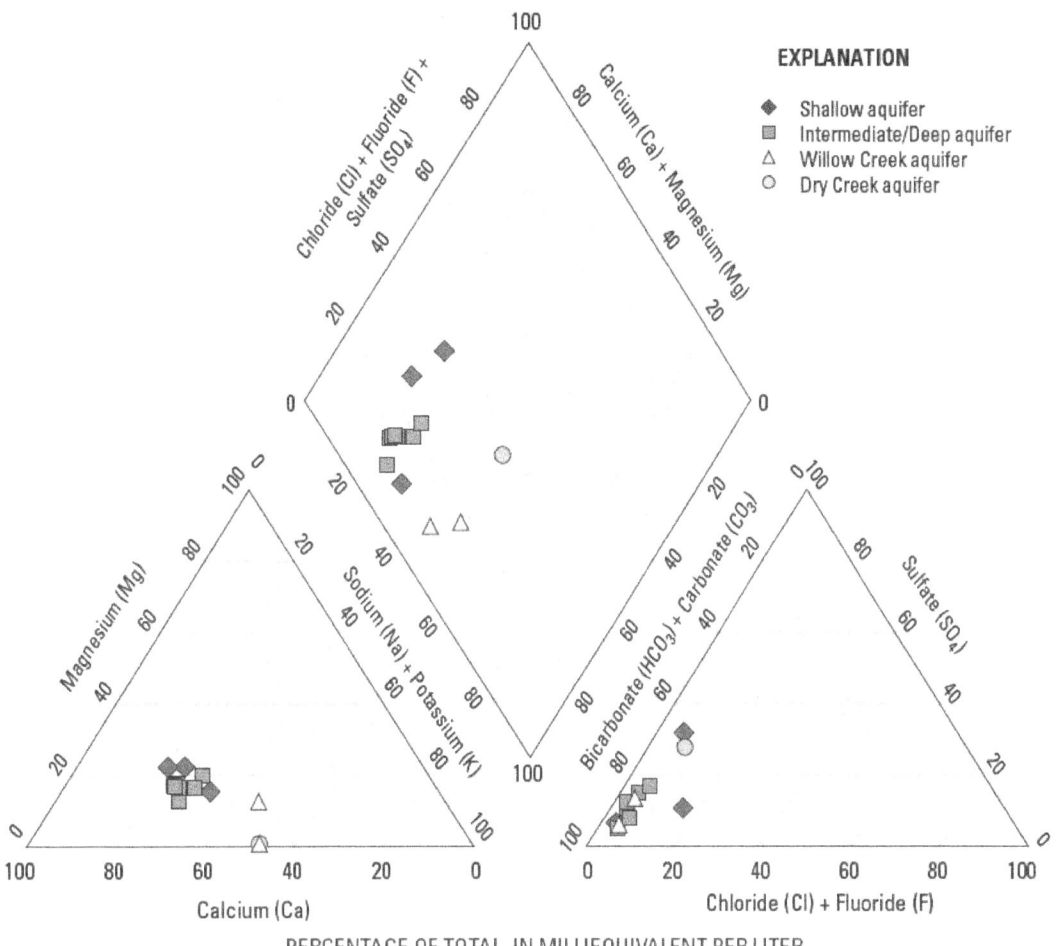

Figure 2. Major ion relations of samples collected from selected wells in northern Ada County, southwestern Idaho, September–October 2009.

Nutrients

Elevated concentrations of nutrients, such as nitrogen and phosphorus, indicate the presence of recharged water affected by human activities (for example, agriculture or wastewater disposal) (Hallberg and Keeney, 1993). An understanding of the sources and sinks of nutrients in groundwater is important because nutrients in high concentrations may have deleterious effects on the environment and on human health. The nutrients sampled for this study were ammonia (as nitrogen), nitrite (as nitrogen), nitrite plus nitrate (as nitrogen), and orthophosphate (as phosphorus).

Ammonia concentrations were detected in samples from the intermediate/deep aquifer, the Willow Creek aquifer, and the Dry Creek aquifer (table 5). Nitrite concentrations were not detected in any of the samples. Nitrite plus nitrate as nitrogen (hereinafter referred to as nitrate) concentrations were highest in shallow aquifer samples (7.01 mg/L); other nitrate concentrations were high (greater than 1.0 mg/L) in intermediate/deep aquifer samples. Orthophosphate concentrations were highest in the intermediate/deep aquifer samples (0.402 mg/L). Orthophosphate was the only nutrient at detectable concentrations in every sample.

Table 5.   Nutrient concentrations for samples collected from selected wells in northern Ada County, southwestern Idaho, September–October 2009.

[Sample name: Location of wells sampled are shown in figure 1. Abbreviations: E, estimated; mg/L, milligrams per liter; <, less than]

Analyte	USGS station No.	Ammonia as N (mg/L)	Nitrite as N (mg/L)	Nitrate+Nitrite as N (mg/L)	Orthophosphate as P (mg/L)
Reporting limit of analyte		0.02	0.002	0.04	0.008
Shallow aquifer					
S1	04N 01E 05BDAC1	<0.02	<0.002	1.76	0.193
S2	04N 01E 06DDD1	<0.02	<0.002	7.01	0.27
S3	05N 01E 34ADCD1	<0.02	<0.002	3.23	0.278
Intermediate/Deep aquifer					
ID1	05N 01W 16DBC1	<0.02	<0.002	<0.04	0.041
ID2	05N 01W 28DDC4	<0.02	<0.002	0.17	0.071
ID3	05N 01W 28DDC5	<0.02	<0.002	2.07	0.402
ID4	04N 01E 14CCB3	0.054	<0.002	<0.04	0.011
ID5	04N 01E 14CCB4	<0.02	<0.002	E 0.02	0.033
ID5R	04N 01E 14CCB4	<0.02	<0.002	E 0.02	0.033
ID6	04N 01E 05CDDD1	<0.02	<0.002	1.36	0.096
ID7	04N 01W 11BDAA1	<0.02	<0.002	<0.04	0.048
Willow Creek aquifer					
WC1	06N 01W 35CCA1	0.062	<0.002	<0.04	0.024
WC2	05N 01W 09CCD2	0.18	<0.002	<0.04	0.153
WC2R	05N 01W 09CCD2	0.18	<0.002	<0.04	0.153
Dry Creek aquifer					
DC1	05N 02E 31ADDD1	<0.02	<0.002	0.77	0.157

Oxygen/Deuterium

The presence and concentrations of oxygen-18 and deuterium (hydrogen-2) in precipitation vary in response to sources of precipitation, altitude, season, temperature, amount of evaporation, and other factors. Thus, oxygen-18 and deuterium can provide information regarding the seasonal timing and altitude of precipitation recharging groundwater. The ratio of oxygen-18 and deuterium to their lighter isotopes (hereinafter referred to as the signature) can indicate changes to water that have occurred since precipitation, such as evaporation or increased water-rock interaction (Coplen, 1993). The Local Meteoric Water Line (LMWL) can be used to describe a continuum in the isotopic signature of local precipitation and its variation from the Global Meteoric Water Line (GMWL) as defined by Craig (1961). For this study, the LMWL representing the Boise area is taken from the modern LMWL as determined by Schlegel and others (2009), with an equation of $\delta^2H=6.94*\delta^{18}O-10.7$.

The results of stable isotope analyses for all samples (table 6) were plotted on a delta diagram along with the modern LMWL as determined by Schlegel and others (2009) and the GMWL as determined by Craig (1961) (fig. 3). Oxygen-18 ($\delta^{18}O$) values ranged from -16.39 to -15.00‰, and deuterium (δ^2H) values ranged from -129 to -119‰. Many of the samples plot below and to the right of the LMWL, displaying a preferential enrichment or excess of oxygen-18 as compared to deuterium relative to the LMWL. Oxygen-18 excess can be a product of evaporation (generating a slope between 3 and 6) or water-rock interaction from low temperature or geothermal waters (increases only the oxygen-18 signature) (Clark and Fritz, 1997). Samples from the foothills aquifers and intermediate/deep aquifer all plot below the LMWL, and two of the shallow aquifer samples (S2, S3) plot below the LMWL.

Table 6. Isotope data for samples collected from selected wells in northern Ada County, southwestern Idaho, September–October 2009.

[Sample name: Location of wells are shown in figure 1. "Modern," indicates water recharged since the 1950s. Abbreviations: ‰, per mil; TU, tritium units; <, less than]

Sample name	USGS station No.	δ^2H H_2O (‰, VSMOW)	$\delta^{18}O$ H_2O (‰, VSMOW)	Tritium (TU)	^{14}C uncorrected (pmc)	$\delta^{13}C$ (‰, VPDB)	Corrected age (years)	Uncorrected age (years)
				Shallow aquifer				
S1	04N 01E 05BDAC1	-124	-16.39	5.8	110.72	-17.84	Modern	Modern
S2	04N 01E 06DDD1	-122	-15.89	5.0	106.08	-17.89	Modern	Modern
S3	05N 01E 34ADCD1	-119	-15.00	4.0	100.31	-15.76	Modern	Modern
				Intermediate/Deep aquifer				
ID1	05N 01W 16DBC1	-124	-15.71	< 0.7	68.33	-13.63	1,900	3,059
ID2	05N 01W 28DDC4	-124	-15.74	< 0.7	81.44	-13.03	1,000	1,649
ID3	05N 01W 28DDC5	-123	-16.00	4.8	102.84	-17.31	Modern	Modern
ID4	04N 01E 14CCB3	-129	-16.59	< 0.7	89.87	-14.07	560	857
ID5	04N 01E 14CCB4	-129	-16.31	6.2	106.78	-16.93	Modern	Modern
ID5R	04N 01E 14CCB4	-129	-16.28	6.0	106.52	-17.20	Modern	Modern
ID6	04N 01E 05CDDD1	-123	-15.95	6.1	102.56	-14.45	Modern	Modern
ID7	04N 01W 11BDAA1	-129	-16.11	< 0.7	74.64	-13.16	1,400	2,350
				Willow Creek aquifer				
WC1	06N 01W 35CCA1	-124	-15.55	< 0.7	35.00	-12.30	8,400	8,433
WC2	05N 01W 09CCD2	-128	-16.12	< 0.7	31.47	-11.73	5,100	9,287
WC2R	05N 01W 09CCD2	-128	-16.12	< 0.7	31.13	-11.80	5,200	9,374
				Dry Creek aquifer				
DC1	05N 02E 31ADDD1	-123	-15.90	1.4	67.02	-13.34	2,000	3,215

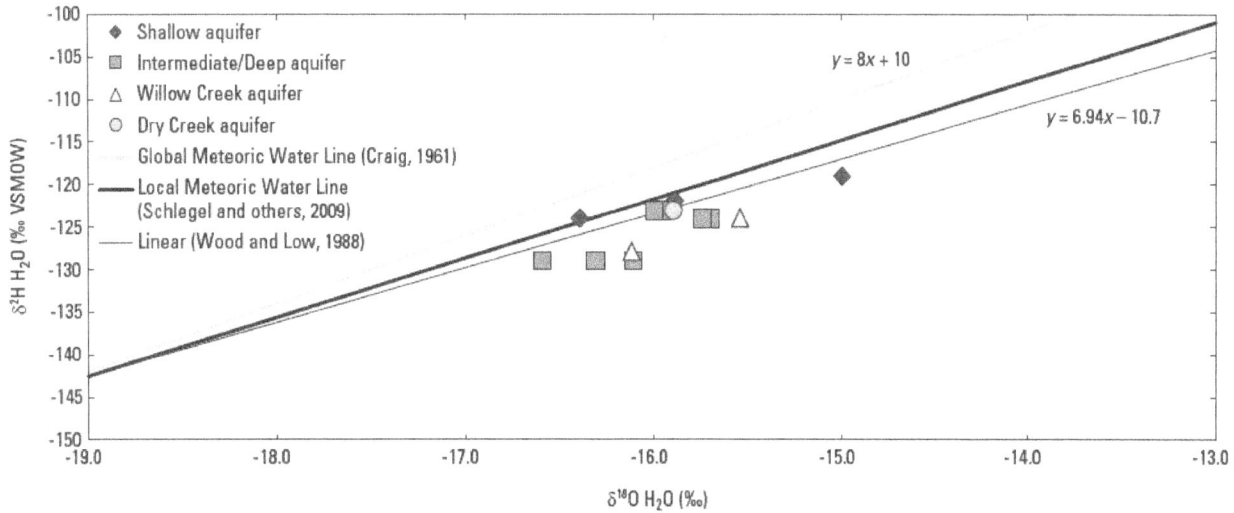

Figure 3. Oxygen and hydrogen isotopes for samples collected from selected wells in northern Ada County with Local Meteoric Water Line and Global Meteoric Water Line, southwestern Idaho, September–October 2009.

Tritium

The short-lived radiogenic isotope tritium, ^{3}H (half-life of 12.43 years), is incorporated into the water molecule during atmospheric contact. It is the only isotope that is capable of dating groundwater itself (Clark and Fritz, 1997). Tritium is produced in small concentrations naturally in the atmosphere by cosmic radiation. However, atmospheric weapons testing between 1951 and 1963 introduced high concentrations that have been used as a means of dating groundwater recharge. The maximum activity of tritium in continental precipitation was approximately 1,000 TU (tritium units) during these years. Tritium activity in pre-1951 recharge water has decayed to less than 0.8 TU, and it was about 8 TU in continental precipitation in Salt Lake City in 2001 (International Atomic Energy Agency, 2001). Tritium incorporated in precipitation can give an estimate of the time that the sample was in contact with the atmosphere; tritium concentrations in samples greater than 0.8 TU indicate modern recharge or mixing with modern waters (Clark and Fritz, 1997). Tritium concentrations in samples less than 0.8 TU are considered to be tritium-dead; they indicate recharge prior to 1951 (Michel, 1989; Plummer and others, 1993; Clark and Fritz, 1997). Analysis of tritium/helium ratios (^{3}H/^{3}He) in groundwater is an ideal tool in systems with piston flow. However, because of the complex nature of the groundwater system in north Ada County and the high likelihood of mixing of water, this analysis was not performed.

Tritium activities throughout northern Ada County ranged from less than 0.7 to 6.2 TU. Tritium activities in samples from the shallow aquifer were 4.0 to 5.8 TU, indicating modern recharge in all samples (table 6). Tritium activities in samples from the intermediate/deep aquifer samples were less than 0.7 to 6.2 TU, with the highest activities in the shallow zones of the monitoring wells (ID3, ID5) and in ID6. The Willow Creek aquifer contained tritium-dead samples with tritium activities of less than 0.7 and 0.4 TU. The sample from the Dry Creek aquifer contained 1.4 TU. Modern water, or some proportion of modern water as determined by tritium activity, was found in samples in the shallow aquifer, intermediate/deep aquifer, and Dry Creek aquifer. Tritium-dead water was found in some of the samples from the intermediate/deep aquifer and in all samples from the Willow Creek aquifer.

Radiocarbon

The primary method of dating groundwater recharge in the 1,000–40,000 year range is carbon-14 (half-life of 5,730 years) dating. Carbon in groundwater is derived from various components of the carbon cycle, and carbon isotopes can give useful information about interactions between groundwater and its environment. Most of the carbon-14 dissolved in groundwater is derived from carbon dioxide present in the soil zone. As recharge water passes through carbon-14 rich dissolved inorganic carbon in the soil zone, it incorporates carbon-14, although carbonate dissolution along a groundwater flowpath may dilute the carbon-14 activity, thereby requiring correction techniques. These techniques may range from the relatively simple (statistical, alkalinity, and carbon-13 mixing model) to advanced geochemical modeling. For this study carbon-13 (measured as δ^{13}C) was measured to evaluate whether significant carbonate dissolution is occurring along the flowpath (Coplen, 1993; Clark and Fritz, 1997).

Carbon-13 (δ^{13}C) results ranged from -17.89 and -11.73‰ throughout the entire system (table 6). The δ^{13}C values ranged from -17.89 to -15.76‰ for the shallow aquifer samples, -17.31 to -13.03‰ for the intermediate/deep aquifer samples, -12.30 to -11.73‰ for the Willow Creek aquifer samples, and the value was -13.34‰ for the Dry Creek aquifer sample. Carbon-13 values were the most positive in samples from the foothills aquifers and were the most negative in the samples from the shallow parts of the aquifer, which suggests that a large portion of dissolved carbon is contributed from soil carbon dioxide. Less negative carbon-13 values may be attributed to increased interaction with the geologic matrix; longer residence times correlated with these more positive carbon-13 values verify this trend (fig. 4).

Carbon-14 values ranged from 31.47 to 110.72 pmc throughout the study area (table 6). Carbon-14 values ranged from 100.31 to 110.72 pmc in samples from the shallow aquifer, and all samples indicated modern recharge. Carbon-14 values ranged from 68.33 to 106.78 pmc in samples from the intermediate/deep aquifer indicating varied residence times. The two samples that indicated modern recharge were from monitoring wells in the intermediate/deep aquifer that were less than 55 ft below land surface that do not experience frequent pumping; the other well indicating modern recharge was deeper than 100 ft and is frequently pumped. Carbon-14 values were lowest in the Willow Creek aquifer samples (31.47–35.00 pmc). The carbon-14 value was 67.02 pmc for the Dry Creek aquifer sample. Uncorrected ages were calculated by the laboratory and were obtained using the decay equation:

$$t = \square 8,267 \ln(a^{14}C / a0^{14}C), \tag{3}$$

where

t is the age of the water sample, in years,

$a^{14}C$ is the measured carbon-14 activity in groundwater, and

$a0^{14}C$ is the carbon-14 activity of water in modern soil (rounded to 100 pmc).

To account for carbonate dissolution and to obtain a more accurate minimum residence time than allowed by simply the decay equation, carbon-14 measurements were corrected using a δ^{13}C mixing model (Clark and Fritz, 1997). The closed system model (developed by Pearson

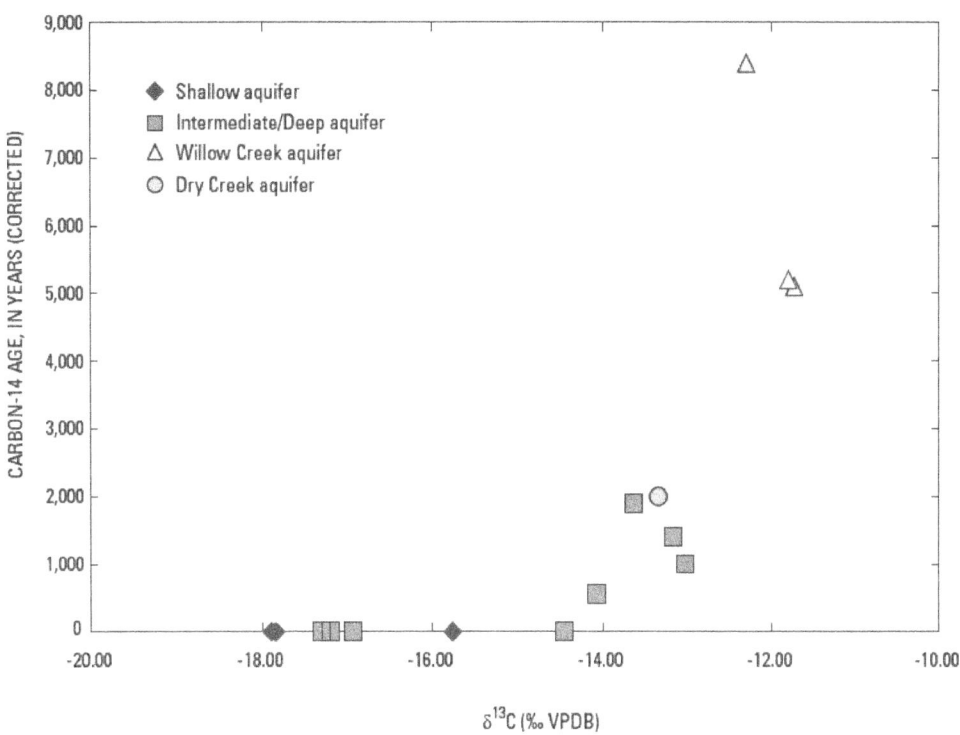

Figure 4.   Carbon-13 values becoming less negative with increasing residence time.

and White, 1967) is a useful tool for correcting carbon-14 age calculations because carbon-13 measurements provide a tracer of carbonate evolution in groundwater. The $\delta^{13}C$ mixing model was used in a similar geochemical study in Treasure Valley, Idaho (Hutchings and Petrich, 2002), and the carbon-13 values they suggested were used for the model in this report. This $\delta^{13}C$ mixing model allows for incorporation of dissolved inorganic carbon during carbonate dissolution, and it accounts for fluctuations in the dissolved-inorganic-carbon pool, which can alter the carbon-14 concentration. This model assumes that carbonate dissolution takes place under closed-system conditions; open-system conditions were not accounted for in this study, but Hutchings and Petrich (2002) suggested that correcting for open-system conditions would result in values similar to the closed system. The $\delta^{13}C$ mixing model-correction factor is calculated using the equation:

$$q = (\delta^{13}C_{DIC} - \delta^{13}C_{carb})/(\delta^{13}C_{soil} - \delta^{13}C_{carb}), \qquad (4)$$

where

   q is the dilution factor,
   $\delta^{13}C_{DIC}$ is the measured $\delta^{13}C$ in groundwater,
   $\delta^{13}C_{carb}$ is the $\delta^{13}C$ of calcite being dissolved, and
   $\delta^{13}C_{soil}$ is the $\delta^{13}C$ of soil carbon dioxide.

Hutchings and Petrich (2002) suggested using 0.0‰ as the $\delta^{13}C$ value of dissolved calcite and -23‰ as the $\delta^{13}C$ value of soil carbon dioxide in the Treasure Valley study. These same values were used in this study.

The correction factor was calculated for each sample and multiplied by the uncorrected age to obtain a corrected age using the following equation from Clark and Fritz (1997):

$$t = \square 8,267 \ln(a^{14}C / q\, a\, 0^{14}C). \qquad (5)$$

Corrected carbon-14 apparent ages (table 6) show the same trends as the uncorrected values. Corrected carbon-14 apparent ages indicate modern water in the shallow aquifer, modern to 1,948 year old water in the intermediate/deep aquifer, 4,847–5,090 year old water in the Willow Creek aquifer, and 2,004 year old water in the Dry Creek aquifer.

Chlorofluorocarbons and Dissolved Gases

Chlorofluorocarbons (CFCs) are stable volatile organic compounds (VOCs) that were first produced in the 1930s for use in refrigeration and that have been used in the production of cleaning solvents, foams, plastics, and other synthetic materials (Clark and Fritz, 1997). CFCs are released into the atmosphere and are stable in the atmosphere. Because historical atmospheric concentrations are known, by measuring concentrations of CFC-12 (dichlorodifluoromethane), CFC-11 (trichlorofluoromethane), and CFC-113 (trichlorotrifluoroethane) in groundwater, it is possible to identify groundwater recharged since about 1941, 1947, and 1955, respectively. Analyses of selected dissolved gases in groundwater (N_2, Ar, CH_4, O_2, and CO_2) provide gas and excess air concentrations, thus allowing estimation of the recharge temperature. Both excess air concentration and recharge temperature are used in the analysis of CFC data to reduce uncertainty in the estimated age. Modeled recharge dates given are based on the time that groundwater entered the aquifer and became isolated from the unsaturated zone (Plummer and others, 1993).

Major dissolved gases were used to determine recharge temperature and to calibrate calculations for CFC data. The calculations involved in determining recharge temperature depended on recharge altitude, thus, a sensitivity analysis for recharge altitude was performed as described below. Two separate analyses were performed for each sample for quality-control purposes. The results indicate the sample name and a lowercase letter for reference, for example S2(a) (table 7). One sample (WC1) was lost during processing, so only one analysis is available at this well. None of the samples were found to have excess nitrogen gas that could skew results; therefore, they did not need to be corrected for this parameter. Estimated recharge temperatures ranged from 41 to 83.3 °F. Reported recharge temperatures are based on recharge occurring 1,000 ft above the land-surface altitude at the well (table 7) because this is the estimated recharge altitude. These recharge temperatures were used for CFC calculations.

Results from CFC analysis (table 8) were calculated based on recharge temperatures and altitudes (table 7). If two different recharge temperatures were generated, the average of the two temperatures was used in the CFC model. Out of the five bottles collected in the field for each CFC analysis, only two or three were analyzed in the laboratory. Results listed in table 8 indicate the sample name and an uppercase letter for reference, for example S2(A). Each CFC-model lists estimated recharge dates and indicates the possibility of contamination. All samples were determined to contain the presence of CFCs; modeled recharge dates range from the late-1940s to the mid-1990s. Dual recharge dates are possible for CFC-11, CFC-12, and CFC-113 due to the turnover in the CFC mixing ratios in the atmosphere (one concentration is equivalent to two different points in time). Although alternative dates are possible for some of the samples collected, the data from all three CFCs were used to calculate the recharge date. Recharge dates for samples in the shallow aquifer fall within the mid-1980s to late-1980s. Samples in the intermediate/deep aquifer indicate recharge from the late-1940s to 1990. Samples in the Willow Creek aquifer indicate recharge from the late-1940s to early 1950s, and the Dry Creek aquifer sample indicates recharge in the early 1960s. In the two monitoring well sites with nested wells (ID2 and ID3, ID4 and ID5), different CFC recharge dates were generated for different depths; older dates correlated with the deeper water.

Because of the complex nature of the groundwater system, recharge altitudes were difficult to determine. Therefore, a sensitivity analysis was used to ascertain how recharge temperature changed over a range of altitudes and, in turn, how this affected CFC results. The minimum recharge altitude used was the altitude of the well, and the maximum altitude used was 7,000 ft (the highest altitude of the Dry Creek drainage basin). The range of recharge altitudes resulted in a maximum temperature difference of 11 °F. The varying recharge temperatures and altitudes were then used in the CFC model. Varying these parameters only slightly affected recharge dates; the greatest difference was only 7 years. Changing recharge altitude and recharge temperature did not, however, affect the overall presence of CFCs, which indicates the presence of modern water in all samples.

Table 7. Dissolved gas data and estimated recharge temperature for samples collected from selected wells in northern Ada County, southwestern Idaho, September–October 2009.

[Well name: Location of wells are shown in figure 1. ft, feet; F, degrees Fahrenheit; cc STP/L, cubic centimeters per liter of pressure at standard temperature and pressure; mm Hg, millimeters of mercury]

Sample name	Legal name	Gases, in milligrams per liter					Assigned recharge altitude (ft)	Recommended recharge temperature (°F)	Excess air (cc STP/L)	Barometric pressure (mm Hg)
		Nitrogen (N$_2$)	Argon (Ar)	Oxygen (O$_2$)	Carbon dioxide (CO$_2$)	Methane (CH$_4$)				
Shallow aquifer										
S1(a)	04N 01E 05BDAC1	22.43	0.7432	4.57	25.01	0.0000	1,097	43.9	5.4	665.9
S1(b)	04N 01E 05BDAC1	22.26	0.7396	4.79	24.98	0.0000	1,097	44.0	5.3	665.9
S2(a)	04N 01E 06DDD1	18.28	0.6586	4.43	66.60	0.0000	1,090	46.8	1.8	666.5
S2(b)	04N 01E 06DDD1	18.21	0.6571	4.41	66.45	0.0000	1,090	46.8	1.7	666.5
S3(a)	05N 01E 34ADCD1	18.84	0.6409	1.13	42.23	0.0000	1,119	52.4	3.6	664.2
S3(b)	05N 01E 34ADCD1	18.87	0.6401	1.39	41.83	0.0000	1,119	52.7	3.6	664.2
Intermediate/Deep aquifer										
ID1(a)	05N 01W 16DBC1	20.05	0.6642	0.23	19.91	0.0000	1,137	51.6	4.7	662.7
ID1(b)	05N 01W 16DBC1	19.94	0.6600	0.24	20.13	0.0000	1,137	52.1	4.7	662.7
ID2(a)	05N 01W 28DDC4	18.76	0.6640	0.99	14.77	0.0000	1,100	47.2	2.4	665.6
ID2(b)	05N 01W 28DDC4	18.88	0.6675	0.99	14.68	0.0000	1,100	46.9	2.5	665.6
ID3(a)	05N 01W 28DDC5	21.67	0.7029	7.56	39.52	0.0000	1,100	49.4	5.8	665.6
ID3(b)	05N 01W 28DDC5	21.72	0.7036	7.08	39.65	0.0000	1,100	49.5	5.9	665.6
ID4(a)	04N 01E 14CCB3	19.23	0.6582	0.24	26.40	0.0000	1,092	50.2	3.5	666.3
ID4(b)	04N 01E 14CCB3	20.23	0.6718	0.50	26.33	0.0000	1,092	51.0	4.7	666.3
ID5(a)	04N 01E 14CCB4	20.28	0.6978	0.26	24.29	0.0078	1,092	45.7	3.6	666.3
ID5(b)	04N 01E 14CCB4	19.95	0.6902	0.26	24.11	0.0068	1,092	46.1	3.4	666.3
ID5R(a)	04N 01E 14CCB4	20.09	0.6947	0.26	24.14	0.0076	1,092	45.7	3.4	666.3
ID5R(b)	04N 01E 14CCB4	20.06	0.6916	0.27	24.05	0.0069	1,092	46.2	3.5	666.3
ID6(a)	04N 01E 05CDDD1	20.23	0.7218	5.55	18.57	0.0000	1,097	41.0	2.5	665.9
ID6(b)	04N 01E 05CDDD1	20.06	0.7171	5.50	18.57	0.0000	1,097	41.3	2.4	665.9
ID7(a)	04N 01W 11BDAA1	19.24	0.6772	0.25	16.05	0.0000	1,070	46.5	2.7	668.0
ID7(b)	04N 01W 11BDAA1	19.12	0.6783	0.25	16.02	0.0000	1,070	45.8	2.4	668.0
Willow Creek aquifer										
WC1(a)	06N 01W 35CCA1	14.35	0.4622	0.17	1.83	0.0070	1177	83.9	3.4	659.6
WC2(a)	05N 01W 09CCD2	15.71	0.5216	0.19	13.63	0.0397	1122	70.7	3.2	663.9
WC2(b)	05N 01W 09CCD2	15.67	0.5210	0.20	13.67	0.0393	1122	70.7	3.1	663.9
WC2R(a)	05N 01W 09CCD2	17.20	0.5465	0.56	14.07	0.0369	1122	70.9	4.7	663.9
WC2R(b)	05N 01W 09CCD2	15.81	0.5240	0.20	13.80	0.0383	1122	70.5	3.3	663.9
Dry Creek aquifer										
DC1(a)	05N 02E 31ADDD1	19.01	0.6500	0.24	12.31	0.0010	1148	50.7	3.5	661.9
DC1(b)	05N 02E 31ADDD1	19.58	0.6623	0.30	12.58	0.0005	1148	50.1	3.9	661.9

Table 8. Chlorofluorocarbon results and modeled groundwater recharge dates for samples collected from selected wells in northern Ada County, southwestern Idaho, September–October 2009.

[Sample name: Location of wells sampled are shown in figure 1. Abbreviations: ft, feet; F, degrees Fahrenheit; pmol/kg, picomole per kilogram; CS, contaminated sample; NP, not possible]

Sample name	Assumed recharge altitude (ft)	Calculated recharge temperature (°F)	Chlorofluorocarbons (pmol/kg)			Model piston dates (excess air corrected)			Recommended age based on	Date recharged
			CFC-11	CFC-12	CFC-113	CFC-11	CFC-12	CFC-113		
Shallow aquifer										
S1(A)	3,600	44.0	2.233	3.301	0.360	1978	1984	1986	CFC-12, CFC-113	Mid 1980s
S1(B)	3,600	44.0	2.212	3.210	0.355	1977	1984	1986		
S2(A)	3,575	46.8	2.402	15.376	0.385	CS	1988	1988	CFC-12, CFC-113	Late 1980s
S2(B)	3,575	46.8	2.340	16.017	0.371	CS	1987	1988		
S2(C)	3,575	46.8	2.380	15.537	0.364	CS	1988	1987		
S3(A)	3,670	52.6	1.815	2.496	0.195	1978	1985	1984	CFC-12, CFC-113	Mid 1980s
S3(B)	3,670	52.6	1.845	2.888	0.206	1980	1986	1984		
Intermediate/Deep aquifer										
ID1(A)	3,730	51.9	0.008	0.161	0.041	1959	1945	1972	CFC-12	Late 1940s to early 1950s
ID1(B)	3,730	51.9	0.008	0.165	0.039	1960	1945	1972		
ID2(A)	3,610	47.1	0.031	0.124	0.014	1957	1949	1963	CFC-12	Late 1940s to early 1950s
ID2(B)	3,610	47.1	0.027	0.126	0.001	1957	1949	1953		
ID2(C)	3,610	47.1	0.035	0.111	0.035	1957	1950	1970		
ID3(A)	3,610	49.5	3.869	4.667	0.226	1988	CS	1984	CFC-11, CFC-113	Mid to late 1980s
ID3(B)	3,610	49.5	3.878	4.713	0.227	1988	CS	1984		
ID4(A)	3,582	50.6	0.031	0.154	0.103	1959	1949	1978	CFC-12	Late 1940s to early 1950s
ID4(B)	3,582	50.6	0.022	0.176	0.064	1960	1948	1975		
ID4(C)	3,582	50.6	1.146	5.719	0.222	CS	1976	1984		
ID5(A)	3,582	45.9	3.492	0.178	1.769	1959	1989	CS	CFC-12	About 1990
ID5(B)	3,582	45.9	2.654	0.179	1.729	1959	1989	CS		
ID5R(A)	3,582	45.9	2.515	0.173	1.562	1959	1989	CS	CFC-12	Mid to late 1980s
ID5R(B)	3,582	45.9	2.150	0.190	1.714	1960	1986	CS		
ID5R(C)	3,582	45.9	1.000	0.138	1.837	1958	1973	CS		
ID6(A)	3,600	41.2	1.607	2.952	0.106	1975	1977	1976	all CFCs	Mid 1970s
ID6(B)	3,600	41.2	1.569	2.584	0.102	1974	1976	1976		
ID6(C)	3,600	41.2	56.373	2.825	0.101	1975	CS	1976		
ID7(A)	3,512	46.7	0.012	0.132	0.032	1957	1946	1969	CFC-12	Late 1940s to early 1950s
ID7(B)	3,512	46.7	0.008	0.131	0.033	1957	1945	1969		

Distribution of Isotopic and Environmental Tracers in Groundwater 19

Table 8. Chlorofluorocarbon results and modeled groundwater recharge dates for samples collected from selected wells in northern Ada County, southwestern Idaho, September–October 2009.—Continued

[Sample name: Location of wells sampled are shown in figure 1. Abbreviations: ft, feet; F, degrees Fahrenheit; pmol/kg, picomole per kilogram; CS, contaminated sample; NP, not possible]

Sample name	Assumed recharge altitude (ft)	Calculated recharge temperature (°F)	Chlorofluorocarbons (pmol/kg)			Model piston dates (excess air corrected)			Recommended age based on	Date recharged
			CFC-11	CFC-12	CFC-113	CFC-11	CFC-12	CFC-113		
Willow Creek aquifer										
WC1(A)	3,860	83.9	0.012	0.207	0.039	1965	1949	1978	CFC-12	Late 1940s to early 1950s
WC1(B)	3,860	83.9	0.015	0.269	0.035	1967	1949	1977		
WC2(A)	3,680	70.7	0.018	0.200	0.101	1963	1949	1983	CFC-12	Late 1940s to early 1950s
WC2(B)	3,680	70.7	0.014	0.156	0.078	1962	1948	1981		
WC2R(A)	3,680	70.7	0.021	0.179	0.085	1963	1950	1981	CFC-12	Late 1940s to early 1950s
WC2R(B)	3,680	70.7	0.017	0.171	0.071	1962	1949	1980		
Dry Creek aquifer										
DC1(A)	3,765	50.4	0.247	0.150	0.044	1959	1963	1972	CFC-12, CFC-11	Early 1960s
DC1(B)	3,765	50.4	0.230	0.155	0.043	1959	1962	1972		
DC1(C)	3,765	50.4	0.213	0.177	0.072	1960	1962	1976		

Application of Tracers in Groundwater

Groundwater flowpaths and flow directions for this study were assumed to follow the three primary flowpaths as determined by Squires (2008). These flowpaths are from the foothills aquifer systems downgradient into the alluvial aquifer system of the Snake River Plain (generally south to southwest), from shallower portions of the alluvial aquifer into deeper portions of the alluvial aquifer, and to a general northwesterly flow in the alluvial aquifer system of the Snake River Plain. A cross section (fig. 5) was constructed by selecting wells along the general flow direction overlain with data from this study highlighting differences in age tracers with depth. Although this cross section does not address geologic influences on groundwater geochemistry, it does demonstrate groundwater age variation at different depths.

Groundwater chemistry near recharge areas reflects the chemistry of recharge sources. As water moves downgradient, it interacts with the aquifer matrix and evolves from its initial chemistry. Groundwater in northern Ada County has a number of recharge sources including precipitation, infiltration of irrigation water, infiltration of canal water, and possibly other surface-water sources. Each of these recharge sources potentially has different water chemistry, which may account for variations in water chemistry and recharge age across the study area. Due to the limited nature of this study, potential recharge sources, such as surface water and precipitation, were not sampled. Thus, changes in chemistry are assumed to be associated only with movement along the groundwater flowpaths.

Major ion chemistry of groundwater (table 4, fig. 2) varies throughout the study area and indicates interaction with local geologic units. Sodium and potassium were

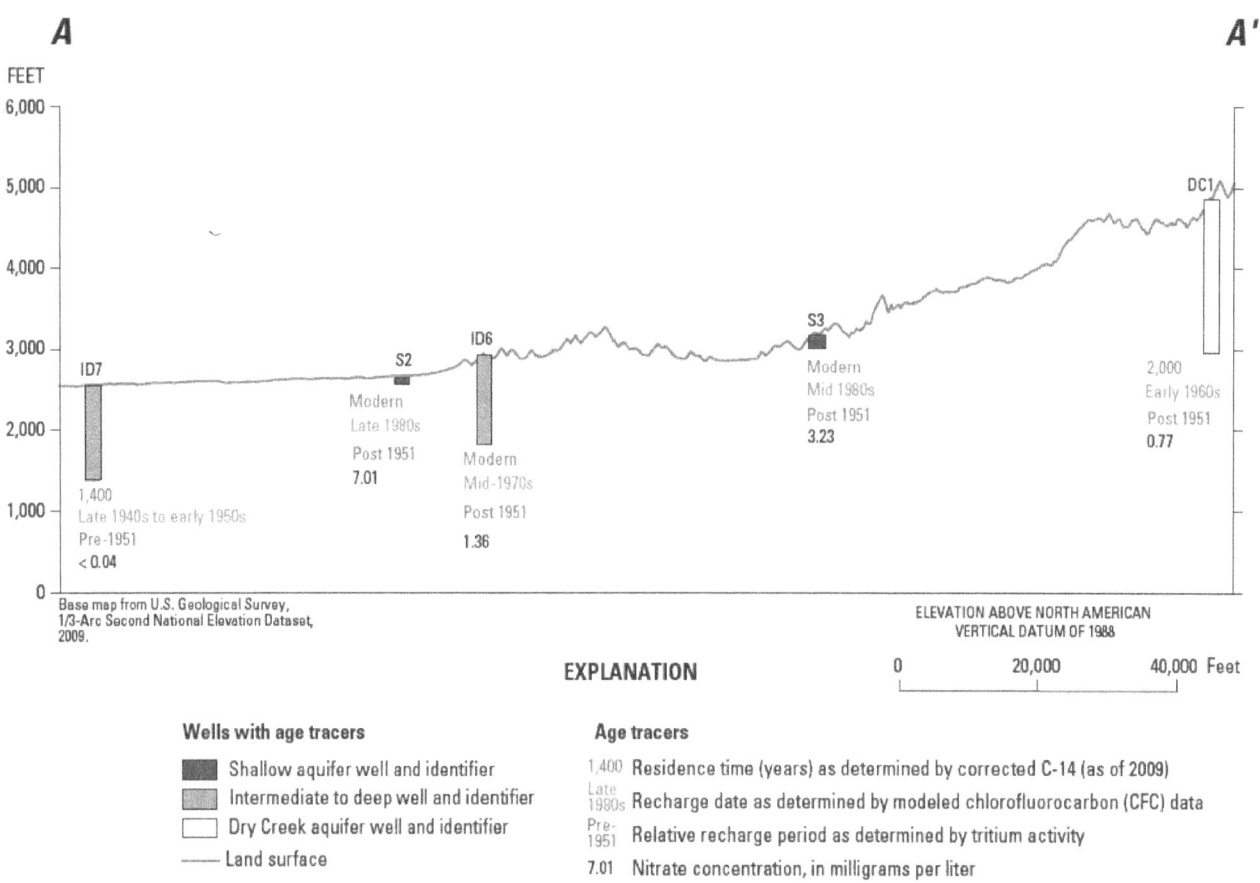

Figure 5.   Age tracers (carbon-14, CFC, tritium, and nitrogen) in samples collected from selected wells in northern Ada County, southwestern Idaho.

combined on the trilinear diagram and in water-type discussions because of their similar chemistry. As water moves downgradient from the foothills aquifers, water type changes from sodium-bicarbonate to calcium-bicarbonate. Samples from differing depths in the Snake River Plain all indicate calcium-bicarbonate type water; samples from the shallow aquifer and the intermediate/deep aquifer are dominated by calcium and bicarbonate. As water moves downgradient from the foothills aquifer systems into the alluvial aquifers, calcium concentrations tend to increase. The geochemical change from the foothills aquifer system could indicate deeper water mixing with water from the shallow aquifer, or dissolution of calcite and other calcium-rich aquifer materials. This geochemical change also could indicate that the foothills aquifers and alluvial aquifers are not hydrologically connected and that they do not allow for geochemical evolution. However, this investigation does not have enough information to address this issue. Due to the possibility of mixing and the complex geology of the alluvial aquifers, neither the exact source of calcium nor the connection between wells can be determined from the samples collected in this study. Additional samples collected from along a discrete flowpath and detailed geologic information could help to determine the source of major ions in groundwater. No distinct trend was determined by silica, iron, and manganese.

High nutrient concentrations in groundwater can be linked to anthropogenic activities, and they are used to help identify modern recharge and its presence throughout a groundwater system. The maximum contamination limit as determined by the EPA is 10 mg/L (U.S. Environmental Protection Agency, 2010). None of the samples in this study had high enough concentrations of nitrate to be near this hazardous level. Concentrations of nitrogen and orthophosphate were highest in samples from the shallow aquifer (table 5, fig. 5), indicating modern recharge. Some samples containing high concentrations of nitrogen and orthophosphate also contain high concentrations of chloride and potassium; evaporation, the application of artificial fertilizers (such as potassium chloride), or influence of septic tanks could explain these high concentrations. Additional samples of recharge water could help to determine if evaporation or application of fertilizers are influencing concentrations in groundwater. Deeper and older age-date waters tended to have low concentrations of both nitrogen and orthophosphate, confirming that high concentrations of these two nutrients reflect more recent recharge.

Oxygen and hydrogen isotopes were analyzed to help elucidate the source of recharge and aquifer interactions in northern Ada County groundwater. Due to the lack of isotopic data for precipitation, variations between seasonal contributions of precipitation could not be determined. Altitude and oxygen (fig. 6A) and hydrogen isotope (fig. 6B) values were plotted against each other to try to determine

if the altitude effect (Clark and Fritz, 1997) contributed to isotopic variation. However, no obvious trend exists indicating that increasing isotope values are correlated with increasing altitude. Carbon-14 results were plotted against oxygen isotopes (fig. 7) to determine if climactic variations due to a changing climate regime affected the stable isotopes or indicated paleorecharge. No trend was apparent; oxygen isotopes have a broad range and more negative values are not correlated with increased age as would be expected from climactic variations.

All but one sample (S1) plotted to the right of the LMWL, indicating oxygen-18 excess or preferential enrichment (fig. 3). Oxygen-18 excess can result from evaporation or water-rock interaction. It is highly likely that this trend is due to evaporation because sources of recharge (inland precipitation and irrigation water) are likely to carry a signature indicating evaporation prior to recharge. However, sources of recharge were not sampled, so the effect of evaporation cannot be determined. Samples showing oxygen-18 excess also could indicate water-rock interaction with geothermal or low-temperature waters (fig. 7). Warmer waters greater than 68°F that could be related to geothermal interaction (Mitchell, 1981) could indicate this trend; many of the geothermal waters along the Boise frontal fault have been proposed to have experienced intense hydrothermal interaction (Schlegel and others, 2009). The three warmer waters greater than 68°F present in this sampling (ID1, WC2, WC1) all show the oxygen-18 excess trend, favoring geothermal interaction as the cause of oxygen-18 excess. Longer residence time leading to increased water-rock interaction also could contribute to oxygen-18 excess. This factor may be considered only if older waters showed this trend. However, samples indicating modern recharge (S2, S3, ID3, ID5) also showed a trend of oxygen-18 excess, inferring that extensive water-rock interaction with low-temperature waters is not the cause of oxygen-18 excess.

Distinct water groups were not defined by oxygen and hydrogen isotopes. Similar isotopic values existed for samples from the shallow aquifer, intermediate/deep aquifer, and foothills aquifers. This similarity could indicate that recharge from the foothills aquifers is contributing to the groundwater system of the intermediate/deep aquifer. No distinct difference was found among aquifer groups, indicating that the groundwater in northern Ada County is complex and well mixed; age dating information, discussed below, also indicates that groundwater is well mixed. Further investigation would help to determine contribution from various recharge sources and potential interactions between aquifer groups. Due to the varied nature of oxygen-18 values and the limited information on isotopic values of recharge sources, oxygen and hydrogen isotopes were not helpful in this study for establishing the source or elevation of recharge, or for mixing of groundwater from different aquifers.

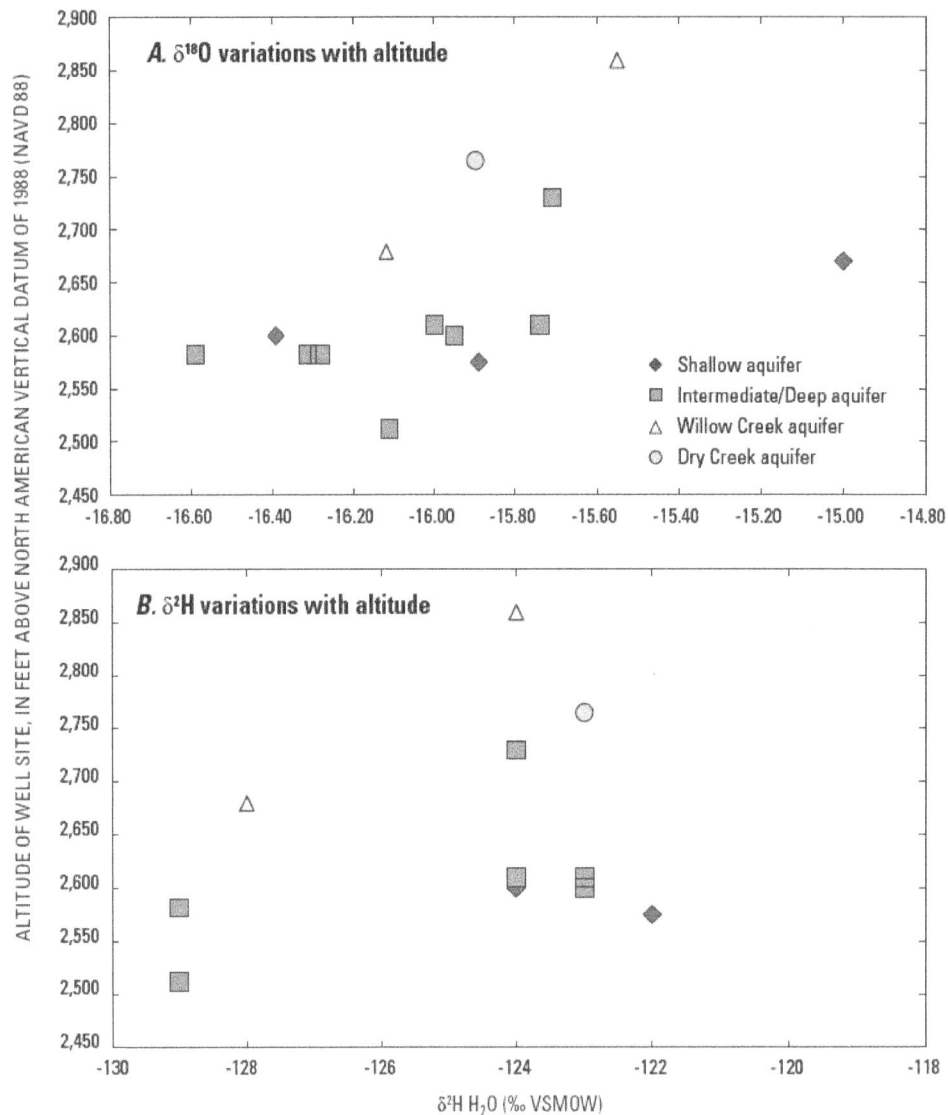

Figure 6.   Variation of (*A*) oxygen isotopes and (*B*) hydrogen isotopes with altitude in samples collected from selected wells in northern Ada County, southwestern Idaho.

Tritium, carbon-14, nutrients, and CFCs are useful age tracers of groundwater residence times, and they can aid in identifying locations of focused recharge. Variations in residence time give insight into flowpaths and recharge areas. Comparing these various age tracers at specific locations (fig. 5) can help in understanding the use of each tracer. Carbon-14 dating generates mean residence time on the scale of thousands of years, whereas CFCs, nutrients, and tritium can detect modern recharge. Groundwater with detectable tritium (greater than 0.7 TU) is indicative of waters recharged within the past 60 years; however, tritium information cannot be used to determine the source of recharge because

precipitation and surface water may be tritium enriched. Tritium can be diluted in a well-mixed system when waters of various age (tritium-enriched modern water, tritium-dead water) blend; therefore, using tritium may not be helpful for identifying areas of modern recharge or for identifying recently recharged waters in the same way as CFC dating.

Tritium activities in northern Ada County (table 6, fig. 5) reveal the presence of modern water in the shallow, intermediate/deep, and Dry Creek aquifers. Modern water (tritium activity greater than 0.8 TU) was found in every sample in the shallow aquifer and the Dry Creek aquifer, indicating that a portion of water in these aquifers has

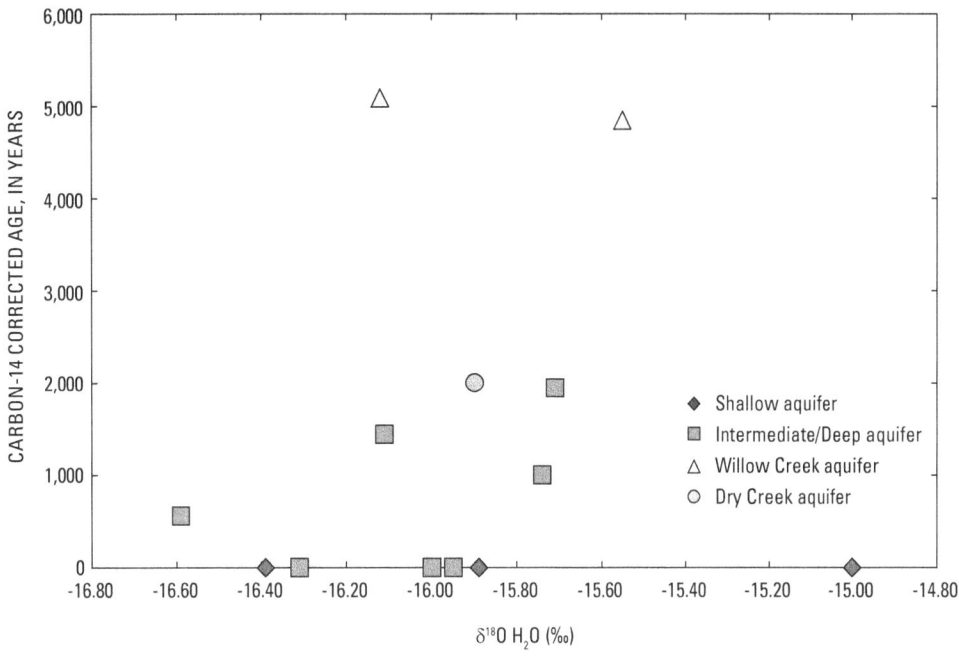

Figure 7. Carbon-14 corrected age and oxygen isotopes in samples collected from selected wells in northern Ada County, southwestern Idaho.

been recharged in the past 60 years. Tritium activities in the intermediate/deep aquifer indicate that some waters have experienced modern recharge, but that some are tritium-dead. Both samples from the Willow Creek aquifer were tritium-dead. Tritium-dead samples either could indicate recharge prior to atomic testing or could imply that tritium has been diluted by mixing. For this study, tritium is best interpreted in conjunction with CFC and carbon-14 data to determine if any modern recharge is occurring.

Analyses of CFCs and dissolved gases indicate that every sample collected in northern Ada County (table 8, fig. 5) contained at least a portion of modern water. Estimated recharge dates generated from CFC modeling ranged from the 1940s to the 1990s. Shallower samples tended to have evidence of more recent recharge; all samples collected at depths less than 180 ft showed evidence of recharge from the mid-1980s or later. Samples in the foothills aquifers show evidence of recharge from the late-1940s to the early 1960s, although recharge dates within the intermediate/deep aquifer vary from the late-1940s to the mid-1970s. CFC results imply that the shallow aquifer has experienced recharge within the past 30 years, although the intermediate/deep aquifer and foothills aquifers have experienced recharge within the past 70 years. Recharge dates indicate older water downgradient from the shallow aquifer, confirming the flowpaths suggested by Squires (2008).

Carbon-14 results indicate varied residence times throughout the system. Groundwater "age" should be thought of as the mean residence times of water molecules sampled because groundwater usually is a mixture of water molecules that recharged at different locations and different times. Carbon-14 dating indicates that samples from the shallow aquifer contain modern recharge, as do the shallow portions from the monitoring wells. Corrected ages in the deeper portion of the deep/intermediate aquifer indicate residence times on the order of 1,000–2,000 years, while the Willow Creek aquifer has residence times around 5,000 years. Carbon-14 residence times imply that older water is present in the study area but because the groundwater seems to be well mixed and only a few samples were taken, it is possible that even older water is present than the corrected dates generated for this study. Residence times tend to increase with depth; variations in residence time along a flowpath could not be determined from this study.

The use of a suite of age tracers confirms age trends in the study area, allowing for insight into the various ages of waters present. Mean residence times tend to increase with depth (fig. 8A), confirming that water flows from shallow to deep portions of the aquifer. This trend is seen somewhat with tritium (fig. 8B) and CFC data (fig. 8C). Young waters, as identified by these tracers, are consistent with elevated concentrations of nutrients (anthropogenic contaminants).

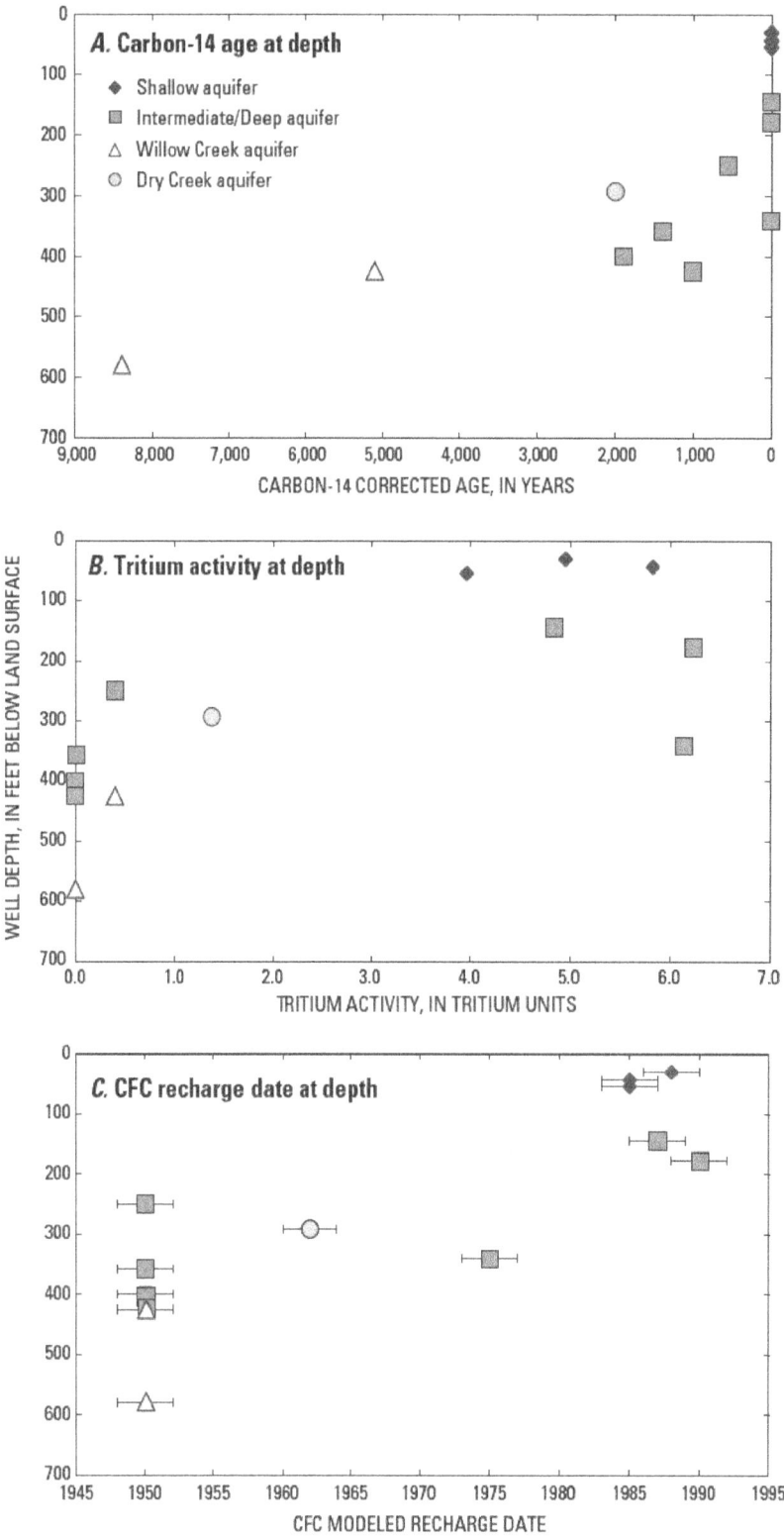

Figure 8.   Age tracers (*A*) carbon-14, (*B*) tritium, and (*C*) chlorofluorocarbons, with depth in samples from northern Ada County, southwestern Idaho.

The presence of CFCs in every sample and tritium in many samples indicates that even samples that have residence times of thousands of years through carbon-14 dating contain at least some modern water. Samples with older carbon-14 ages also have older recharge dates as determined by CFC dating, indicating that this modern water took years to reach this portion of the aquifer. Similarly, comparing concentrations of tritium and radiocarbon (fig. 9) indicates that age tracers are in agreement and are able to identify relatively younger or older waters. No distinct pattern is seen between solute chemistry data and ages as determined by carbon-14 dating.

Mixing is likely to occur due to the highly permeable and interbedded composition of the aquifers in this study. The presence of young and old waters in the same sample indicates a well-mixed groundwater system that has the potential for infiltration of young water into older groundwater. Modern recharge typically is dominant in shallower samples, and it

was found in every sample in the study. However, carbon-14 dating indicates that samples that have experienced modern recharge may also have a mean residence time of up to thousands of years. These older residence times are typical of deeper samples in the study area and, they could be a product of depth or compartmentalization. The varying age dates indicate that some areas of the intermediate/deep aquifer have complex recharge systems and that these systems experience focused but relatively small volumetric modern recharge. Some areas of the intermediate/deep aquifer (ID6) and the entire shallow aquifer seem to be dominated by modern recharge. Due to the small number of samples collected for this study, geochemical changes along a flowpath or with increased residence time are difficult to determine. Similarly, determination of sources of recharge was difficult due to lack of data about recharge sources.

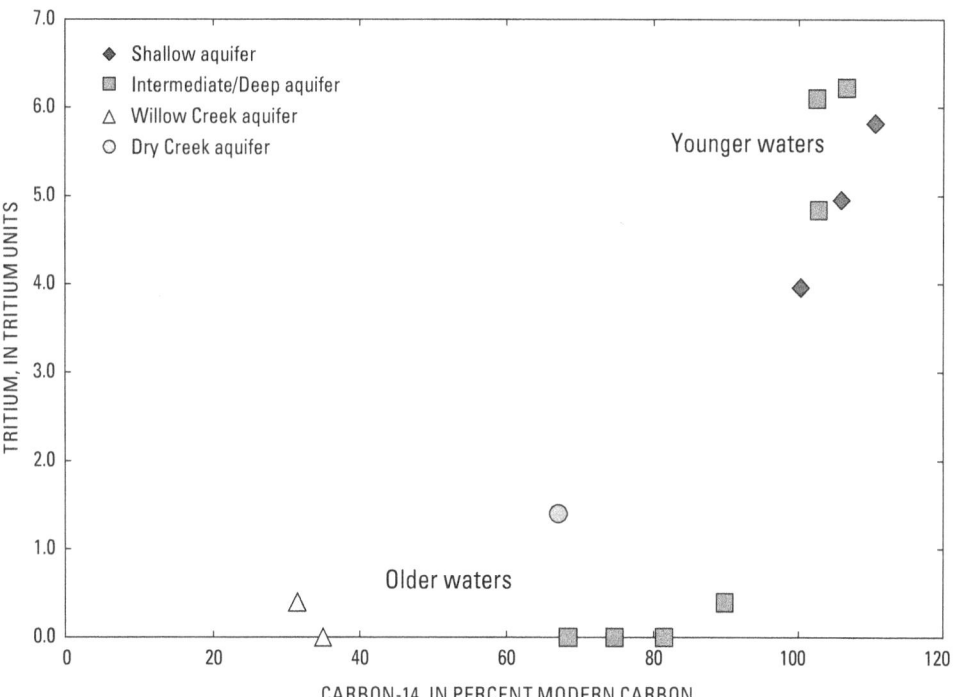

Figure 9. Tritium concentration and carbon-14 activity in samples collected from selected wells in northern Ada County, southwestern Idaho.

Suggestions for Further Study

Future geochemical studies involving the isotopic tracers used in this study could help to improve understanding of the hydrologic system of northern Ada County. More samples spanning a larger area and taken from various depths could help to determine regional groundwater trends. Future sampling strategies should aim to collect a large number of samples and target samples from wells close to one another and in the same stratigraphic unit to determine geochemical changes along a determined flowpath. Future sampling efforts also should aim to stratify well selection by various anthropogenic contaminants (such as septic system density or fertilizer application intensity) to help determine sources of anthropogenic compounds. In addition, more samples need to be obtained from the foothills aquifers to understand the hydraulic connectivity between these aquifers and those in the Snake River Plain. Sampling monitoring wells at various depths proved to be a useful technique in this study and should be utilized in future studies.

Although major ion chemistry did not add to the understanding of the system in this study, collecting major ion chemistry of source waters in addition to that of groundwater could help to elucidate sources of recharge to the system. Geochemical modeling can use saturation indices to help to identify minerals that groundwater interacts with and the trend of chemical evolution that groundwater experiences. Saturation indices for samples collected for northern Ada County study were examined along an assumed flowpath to determine major geochemical reactions; however, no consistent patterns were recognized, possibly because of the varied nature of the aquifer matrix and interactions between aquifers. In future studies, saturation indices may be used to examine major geochemical reactions expected along flowpaths and may yield further insight into the groundwater system.

Future studies also could include sampling oxygen and hydrogen isotopes of recharge sources to assess recharge sources and chemical evolution of recharge water. Oxygen and hydrogen isotopes of precipitation and source water (such as the Boise River, canals, and urban irrigation sources) should be collected at various altitudes and throughout various seasons to assess altitude and seasonality of recharge so as to account for evaporation, altitude, and seasonal effects. Sampling for oxygen and hydrogen isotopes also could help to determine whether the oxygen-18 excess trend seen in this study is attributed to recharge from evaporated sources or water-rock interaction.

Understanding of the system was improved by including age tracers in this study; future studies should include age-dating techniques, but can minimize the number of methods used while still gaining useful information. Nutrient, CFC, and tritium data all were used to identify modern waters, and they detected similar trends. Because tritium can be diluted in a well-mixed system, and because tritium analyses are expensive, it may not be the best tool for detecting modern recharge. Similarly, nutrient data can be diluted easily and is not always found in modern recharge. Nutrient data also are highly sensitive to redox conditions and nitrate concentrations can be lowered by reducing conditions. For this study area involving mixed groundwaters, CFC analyses were the most useful tracer of modern water because this tracer does not decay, can be detected in small amounts, and is evenly distributed across the study area. In similar study areas, especially in a similar region with well-mixed groundwater, CFC age-dating techniques may be the most cost-effective and efficient indicator of modern recharge.

In addition, age-dating techniques that were used in this study could be improved in a number of ways for more accurate dating in future studies. If tritium activities are sampled in the future, analyzing tritium activities in local precipitation could help to refine the relative age of recharge. Carbon-14 age estimates could be improved by constraining the age correction model used in this study. Soil and carbonate $\delta^{13}C$ values were approximated for this study and were taken from previous modeling efforts. The values of $\delta^{13}C$ in local soil and carbonate samples could help to constrain the $\delta^{13}C$ mixing model correction model, and decrease error in carbon-14 age estimates.

Summary and Conclusions

In this study, general chemistry and geochemical tracers were measured from a group of wells in northern Ada County to understand the groundwater-flow system. Isotopic and environmental tracer data were collected from 13 wells at 11 sites, and the data were used to determine geochemical relations and relative recharge dates of the groundwater.

Major-ion chemistry was able to determine a shift in water type from the foothills aquifers (sodium-bicarbonate) into the plains aquifers (calcium-bicarbonate). However, due to the limited number of samples, lack of data about source waters, and minimal geologic information about the study area, the source of this water type change could not be identified. Major-ion chemistry did not seem to provide any information that could be used to determine relations between aquifer groups, relative recharge date of water, source of water, or geochemical evolution of water. In future studies, major-ion chemistry may be useful if samples of source water and additional groundwater samples can be obtained and saturation indices are examined. In addition, simple mixing models may help to explain the dominance of certain ions. In this study, however, major ion chemistry did not contribute significantly to the overall understanding of the groundwater system.

Nutrient data in this study helped to identify samples that have elevated concentrations of nitrate and orthophosphate and that have most likely experienced modern recharge. Shallow samples seemed to have high concentrations of nitrate, indicating that they had been evaporated or recharged from modern waters. Although this method is not able to give an approximate date of recharge, sampling for nutrient data indicates recharge that has occurred during the use of modern agricultural practices or during urban development. Modern water, as determined by nutrient data, generally agreed with water dated with tritium and CFC analyses. However, nutrient data did not identify all modern recharge as determined by these methods. Nutrient analysis may not always identify modern recharge (especially if there is little agriculture), but it is a low-cost alternative to age-dating.

Oxygen and hydrogen isotopes indicated a pattern of oxygen-18 excess, signaling that groundwater within the study area has experienced either evaporation before recharge or water-rock interaction. However, due to the lack of oxygen and hydrogen isotope information for recharge sources, the cause of this trend could not be determined. Conclusions about recharge sources or recharge environment could not be determined by oxygen and hydrogen data. Without further sampling of source waters, oxygen and hydrogen isotopes are not helpful in determining relations between water groups or in identifying sources of recharge. However, if further studies are conducted and sources of water are sampled, oxygen and hydrogen isotopes may prove to be a useful method of determining the source of recharge to the system or of waters that may have had geothermal interaction.

Tritium data indicated that modern to older, tritium-dead water existed in northern Ada County. Tritium activities generally agreed with age dates as determined by CFCs and carbon-14 dating, indicating that modern recharge is occurring in the shallow aquifer, portions of the intermediate/deep aquifer, and in the Dry Creek aquifer, although older (tritium-dead) samples were found in the intermediate/deep aquifer and in the Willow Creek aquifer. Due to the similar range of age dates generated by tritium and CFC data analyses and the relatively high expense of these analyses, it would be logical to perform only one of these analyses. No sampling or field constraints would prefer one analysis to another. However, this study has shown that groundwater in northern Ada County is well-mixed and could dilute tritium activity in water; some samples showed modern water as indicated by CFCs but not by tritium, possibly due to dilution or radioactive decay. To gain the most accurate information about modern recharge, CFC dating would be preferred over tritium dating.

Dissolved gas and CFC data determined that modern water was present in every single well sampled in this study. These data, coupled with carbon-14 and tritium data, indicate that water molecules of different ages exist in the same portion of an aquifer. The discrepancies among the recharge ages indicate that the system is well-mixed, but that, in general, older water tends to be deeper in the system and younger water tends to be shallower in the system. In addition, CFC data confirmed assumed groundwater flowpaths of water moving downward into the system from shallower portions of the aquifer. Measuring for CFCs and dissolved gases was helpful in identifying the presence of modern recharge throughout the system, and this technique should be used in future studies in northern Ada County. However, only when CFC data were coupled with carbon-14 data was it apparent that the system was well-mixed; future studies should include both of these tracers for identification of mixed groundwater.

Groundwater in northern Ada County had recharge dates of thousands of years ago to modern recharge through carbon-14 dating. In this study, carbon-14 dates were corrected using the carbon-13 mixing model. In future studies, collecting for carbon-13 and carbon-14 isotopes would be helpful in constraining recharge dates. Sampling local carbonate and soil CO_2 could help to produce more accurate age estimates. Carbon-14 is helpful in indicating that old water does exist in the system and that it may make up a significant amount of the available water in the aquifer.

This study is limited in its conclusions due to the limited amount of data collected; although it was able to determine that the northern Ada County study area contains well-mixed groundwater that has been recharged by modern and older water. Sources of recharge and complex relations among aquifers were unable to be assessed with certainty. To establish sources of recharge more accurately, additional samples would need to be collected.

Acknowledgments

The authors thank Dennis Owsley and Sean Vincent of IDWR; Ed Squires and Loren Pearson of Hydro Logic, Inc.; Roger Dittus of United Water; Deb Parliman, Jim Schaeffer, Alvin Sablan, and Rhonda Weakland of the USGS; and the landowners who gave us permission to sample their wells.

References Cited

Back, William, 1966, Hydrochemical facies and ground-water flow patterns in northern part of Atlantic Coastal Plain: U.S. Geological Survey Professional Paper 498-A, 42 p.

Baker, S.J., 1991, Ground-water conditions in the Dry Creek area, Eagle, Idaho: Boise, ID, Idaho Department of Water Resources, 27 p., accessed June 17, 2010, at http://www.idwr.idaho.gov/WaterInformation/Publications/ofr/ofr-gw_conditions_drycr_eagle_id.pdf.

Berenbrock, Charles, 1997, Streamflow gains and losses in the lower Boise River basin, Idaho, 1996–97: U.S. Geological Survey Water-Resources Investigations Report 99-4105, 25 p.

Bureau of Reclamation, 2006, AgriMet—The Pacific Northwest Cooperative Agricultural Weather Network—AgriMet network map: Accessed Jan. 3, 2010, at http://www.usbr.gov/pn/agrimet/agrimetmap/agrimap.html.

Church, John, 2007, Economic and population forecasts for Ada and Canyon Counties in Idaho (2007–2040): Boise, ID, Idaho Economics, prepared for the Community Planning organization of Southwest Idaho (COMPASS), 87 p., accessed June 17, 2010, at http://www.compassidaho.org/documents/prodserv/demo/JohnChurchForecast.pdf.

Clark, I.D., and Fritz, Peter, 1997, Environmental isotopes in hydrogeology: Boca Raton, New York, Lewis Publishers, 328 p.

Coplen, T.B., 1993, Uses of environmental isotopes, in Alley, W.M., ed., Regional ground-water quality: New York, Van Nostrand Reinhold, p. 227–254.

Coplen, T.B., 1996, New guidelines for reporting stable hydrogen, carbon, and oxygen isotope-ratio data: Geochemica et Cosmochimica Acta, v. 60, issue 17, p. 3359–3360.

Coplen, T.B., Wildman, J.D., and Chen, Julie, 1991, Improvements in the gaseous hydrogen-water equilibration technique for hydrogen isotope ratio analysis: Analytical Chemistry, v. 63, pp. 910–912.

Craig, Harmon, 1961, Isotopic variations in meteoric waters: Science, v. 133, no. 3465, pp. 1702–1703.

Dion, N.P., 1972, Some effects of land use changes on the shallow ground water system in the Boise–Nampa area, Idaho: Idaho Department of Water Resources Water Information Bulletin 26, 47 p.

Fishman, M.J., ed., 1993, Methods of analysis by the U.S. Geological Survey National Water Quality Laboratory—Determination of inorganic and organic constituents in water and fluvial sediments: U.S. Geological Survey Open File Report 93-125, 217 p.

Fishman, M.J., and Friedman, L.C., eds., 1989, Methods for determination of inorganic substances in water and fluvial sediments: U.S. Geological Survey Techniques of Water-Resources Investigations, book 5, chap. A1, 545 p. (Also available at http://pubs.water.usgs.gov/twri5a1.)

Glanzman, R.K., and Squires, Edward, 2009, Ground water geochemistry of wells in the north Ada County area of Idaho: Boise, ID, Hydro Logic, Inc., Technical Memorandum, Jan. 20, 2009, 11 p., accessed June 17, 2010, at http://www.idwr.idaho.gov/WaterInformation/Projects/nac/consultant_reports/M3/Supporting%20Documentation%20for%20Water%20Right%2063-32573/1-20-2009%20Final%20Geochemistry%20Technical%20Memorandum.pdf.

Godfrey, Bruce, 2000, Köppen climate classification for the conterminous United States: Accessed Jan. 3, 2010, at http://snow.cals.uidaho.edu/Clim_Map/koppen_usa_map.htm.

Hallberg, G.R., and Keeney, D.R., 1993, Nitrate, in Alley, W.M., ed., Regional ground-water quality: New York, Van Nostrand Reinhold, pp. 297–322.

Hardy, M.W., 2008, Quality-assurance plan for water-quality activities for the U.S. Geological Survey Idaho Water Science Center: Accessed June 17, 2010, at http://id.water.usgs.gov/usgs/science/qwqa/QW_QAplan_2008.pdf.

Hill, R.A., 1940, Geochemical patterns in Coachella Valley, California: Transactions, American Geophysical Union, v. 21, p. 46–53.

Holdaway, B., 1994, The geochemical evolution of cold and thermal ground waters in the southern part of the Idaho Batholith: Provo, Utah, Brigham Young University, Masters Thesis, 73 p.

Hutchings, Jon, and Petrich, C.R., 2002, Ground water recharge and flow in the regional Treasure Valley aquifer system, geochemistry and isotope study: Boise, ID, Water Resources Research Institute, Research Report IWRRI-2002-08, 80 p., accessed June 17, 2010, at http://www.idwr.idaho.gov/WaterInformation/Projects/nac/consultant_reports/M3/Supporting%20Documentation%20for%20Water%20Right%2063-32573/33%20%5B07%5D%20TVHP_Geochemistry-final.pdf.

International Atomic Energy Agency, 2001, Isotope Hydrology Information System: The ISOHIS database, accessed June 17, 2010, at http://www-naweb.iaea.org/na/index.html.

Mariner, R.H., Young, H.W., Parliman, D.J., and Evans, W.C., 1989, Geochemistry of thermal water from selected wells, Boise, Idaho, *in* The Geysers — Three decades of achievement: Geothermal Resources Council Transactions, v. 13, p. 173–178.

Mayo, A.L., Muller, A.B., and Mitchell, J.C., 1984, Geothermal investigations in Idaho: Geochemical and isotopic investigations of thermal water occurrences of the Boise front area, Ada County, Idaho: Idaho Department of Water Resources Water Information Bulletin 30, pt. 14, 60 p.

Mitchell, J., 1981, Geological, hydrological, geochemical, and geophysical investigations of the Nampa-Caldwell and adjacent areas, southwestern Idaho: Idaho Department of Water Resources Water Information Bulletin 30, pt. 11, 143 p.

Natural Resources Conservation Service, 2010, Idaho Snow Survey Program: Accessed Jan. 3, 2010, at http://www.id.nrcs.usda.gov/snow/.

Neely, K.W., and Crockett, J.K., 1998, Ground water quality characterization and initial trend analyses for the Treasure Valley shallow and deep hydrogeologic subareas: Idaho Department of Water Resources Water Information Bulletin 50, pt. 3, 76 p., 5 apps., accessed June 17, 2010, at http://www.idwr.idaho.gov/WaterInformation/Publications/wib/wib50p3-gwq_treasure_valley.pdf.

Newton, G.D., 1991, Geohydrology of the regional aquifer system, western Snake River Plain, southwestern Idaho: U.S. Geological Survey Professional Paper 1408-G, p. G1-G52, 1 pl.

Parliman, D.J., 1982, Compilation of ground-water quality data for selected wells in Elmore, Owyhee, Ada, and Canyon Counties, Idaho, 1945 through 1982: U.S. Geological Survey Open-File Report 83-39, 156 p. (Also available at http://pubs.er.usgs.gov/usgspubs/ofr/ofr8339.)

Parliman, D.J., Boyle, Linda, and Nicholls, Sabrina, 1996, Selected well and ground-water chemistry data for the Boise River Valley, southwestern Idaho, 1990–95: U.S. Geological Survey Open-File Report 96-246, 199 p. (Also available at http://pubs.er.usgs.gov/usgspubs/ofr/ofr96246).

Parliman, D.J., and Spinazola, J.M., 1998, Ground-water quality in northern Ada County, lower Boise River basin, Idaho, 1985–96: U.S. Geological Survey Fact Sheet 054-98, 6 p. (Also available at http://pubs.er.usgs.gov/usgspubs/fs/fs05498.)

Parliman, D.J., and Young, H.W., 1992, Compilation of selected data for thermal-water wells and springs in Idaho, 1921 through 1991: U.S. Geological Survey Open-File Report 92-175, 201 p.

Pearson, F.J., Jr., and White, D.E., 1967, Carbon-14 ages and flow rates of water in the Carrizo Sand, Atascosa County, Texas: Water Resources Research, v. 3, no. 1, p. 251–261.

Peel, M.C., Finlayson, B.L., and McMahon, T.A., 2007, Updated world map of the Köppen-Geiger climate classification: Hydrology and Earth System Sciences, v. 11, p. 1633–1644, accessed Jan. 3, 2010, at http://www.hydrol-earth-syst-sci.net/11/1633/2007/hess-11-1633-2007.pdf.

Piper, A.M., 1944, A graphic procedure in the geochemical interpretation of water analyses: Transactions, American Geophysical Union, v. 25, p. 914–923.

Plummer, L.N., Michel, R.L., Thurman, E.M., and Glynn, P.D., 1993, Environmental tracers for age-dating young ground water, *in* Alley, W.M., ed., Regional ground-water quality: New York, Van Nostrand Reinhold, p. 255–294.

Révész, Kinga, and Coplen, Tyler, B., 2008a, Determination of the $\delta(^{18}O/^{16}O)$ of water: RSIL lab code 489, chap. C2 of Révész, Kinga, and Coplen, Tyler B., eds., Methods of the Reston Stable Isotope Laboratory: U.S. Geological Survey Techniques and Methods, 10–C2, 28 p. (Also available at http://pubs.usgs.gov/tm/2007/tm10c2/.)

Révész, Kinga, and Coplen, T.B., 2008b, Determination of the $\delta(^{2}H/^{1}H)$ of water: RSIL lab code 1574, chap. C1 of Révész, Kinga, and Coplen, T.B., eds., Methods of the Reston Stable Isotope Laboratory: U.S. Geological Survey Techniques and Methods 10–C1, 27 p. (Also available at http://pubs.usgs.gov/tm/2007/tm10c1/.)

Schlegel, M.E., Mayo, A.L, Nelson, Steve, Tingey, Dave, Henderson, Rachel, and Eggett, Dennis, 2009, Paleo-climate of the Boise area, Idaho from the last glacial maximum to the present based on groundwater $\delta^{2}H$ and $\delta^{18}O$ compositions: Quaternary Research, v. 71, issue 2, p. 172–180.

SPF Water Engineering, LLC, 2004, Aquifer evaluation in the Big Gulch and Little Gulch areas of Spring Valley Ranch: Boise, Idaho, SPF Water Engineering, LLC. Report prepared for SunCor Development Company, 23 p., 6 apps., accessed June 17, 2010, at http://www.idwr.idaho.gov/WaterInformation/Projects/nac/consultant_reports/Avimor/Aquifer%20Evaluation%2010_2004.pdf.

Squires, Edward, 2008, Surveyed water level measurements of wells in the northern Ada County/Eagle area, for the M3 Eagle hydrogeologic characterization: Boise, Idaho, Hydro Logic, Inc., Technical memorandum, March 17, 2008, accessed June 17, 2010, at http://www.idwr.idaho.gov/WaterInformation/projects/nac/consultant_reports/M3/HydroLogicInc-Water_Level_Measurement_Survey_Update_to_M3_Eagle_Hydrogeologic_Characterization.pdf.

Squires, Edward, Utting, M., and Pearson, L., 2007, M3 Eagle regional hydrogeologic characterization—north Ada, Canyon and Gem Counties, Idaho—year-one progress report: Boise, ID, Hydro Logic, Inc., consultant's report issued May 4, 2007.

Squires, Edward, and Wood, S.H., 2001, Stratigraphic studies of the Boise (Idaho) aquifer system using borehole geophysical logs *with emphasis on* facies identification of sand aquifers: Report to the Idaho Department of Water Resources, prepared for the Treasure Valley Hydrologic Study, 16 p.

Urban, S.M., 2004, Water budget for the Treasure Valley aquifer for the years 1996 and 2000, Treasure Valley Hydrologic Project—Research report: Boise, ID, Idaho Department of Water Resources Research Report.

U.S. Census Bureau, 2009, Population of counties by decennial census: 1900 to 1990: Compiled and edited by Richard Forstall, Population Division, accessed May 18, 2009, at http://www.census.gov/population/cencounts/id190090.txt.

U.S. Department of Agriculture, 2010, Common land use GIS database: Salt Lake City, UT, Created by USDA-FSA Aerial Photography Office, series number 20051107.

U.S. Department of Commerce, 2010, National Climatic Data Center: Accessed Jan. 26, 2010, at http://www ncdc noaa. gov.

U.S. Environmental Protection Agency, 2010, Basic information about nitrate in drinking water: Accessed April 27, 2010, at http://www.epa.gov/safewater/contaminants/basicinformation/nitrate.html.

U.S. Geological Survey, variously dated, National field manual for the collection of water-quality data: U.S. Geological Survey Techniques of Water-Resources Investigations, book 9, chaps. A1–A9. (Also available at http://pubs.water. usgs.gov/twri9A.)

U.S. Geological Survey, 2006. The Reston Chlorofluorocarbon Laboratory, dissolved gas sampling instructions: Accessed June 17, 2010, at http://water.usgs.gov/lab/dissolved-gas/sampling/.

U.S. Geological Survey, 2009, The Reston Chlorofluorocarbon Laboratory, CFC sampling method—Bottles: Accessed June 17, 2010, at http://water.usgs.gov/lab/chlorofluorocarbons/sampling/bottles/.

U.S. Geological Survey, 2010a, National Water Information System (NWISWeb)—USGS Water-Quality Data for Idaho: U.S. Geological Survey database, accessed June 17, 2010, at http://waterdata.usgs.gov/id/nwis/qw.

U.S. Geological Survey, 2010b, Isotope Tracers Project—Stable isotope and tritium labs: Accessed June 17, 2010, at http://wwwrcamnl.wr.usgs.gov/isoig/bios/capabilities.html.

Western Regional Climate Center, 2008, Idaho climate summaries: Accessed Jan. 3, 2010, at http://www.wrcc.dri.edu/summary/climsmid.html.

Wood, S.H., 1994, Seismic expression and geological significance of a lacustrine delta in Neogene deposits of the western Snake River Plain, Idaho: American Association of Petroleum Geologists Bulletin, v. 78, p. 102–121.

Wood, S.H., and Anderson, J.E., 1981, Geology, *in* Mitchell, J.C., ed., Geothermal investigations in Idaho, part 11, Geological, hydrological, geochemical, and geophysical investigations of the Nampa-Caldwell and adjacent areas, southwestern Idaho: Idaho Department of Water Resources Water Information Bulletin 30, p. 9–31.

Wood, S.H., and Clemens, D.M., 2002, Geologic and tectonic history of the western Snake River Plain, Idaho and Oregon, *in* Bonnichsen, Bill, White, C.M., and McCurry, Michael, eds., Tectonic and magmatic evolution of the Snake River Plain volcanic province: Moscow, ID, Idaho Geological Survey Bulletin 30, pp. 69–103.

Wood, W.W., and Low, W.H., 1988, Solute geochemistry of the Snake River plain regional aquifer system, Idaho and eastern Oregon: U.S. Geological Survey Professional Paper 1408-D, 79 p. (Also available at http://pubs.er.usgs.gov/usgspubs/pp/pp1408D.

Woods Hole Oceanographic Institution, 2003, Measuring ^{14}C in seawater ΣCO_2 by accelerator mass spectrometry: Woods Hole, MA, WHP Operations and Methods, July 2003, 9 p., accessed June 17, 2010, at http://www.nosams.whoi.edu/docs/Water%20sampling%20protocol.doc.

www.ingramcontent.com/pod-product-compliance
Lightning Source LLC
Chambersburg PA
CBHW081803280526
45789CB00008B/2982

* 9 7 8 1 5 0 0 5 0 5 0 4 2 *